PRAISE FOR *L*

In this immensely engaging book, Sonny Magana provides a new view of the learner that goes well beyond the traditional perspective of "receiver of information." His concept of meta-learning has the potential to set the foundations for the new pedagogy of the twenty-first century.

—**Robert J. Marzano**, founder and chief academic officer, Marzano Resources

I absolutely loved this book! *Learning in the Zone* is a must-read for all educators. Once again, Sonny Magana has found a way to provide a simple presentation for sophisticated ideas as he takes the reader through his own learning journey and weaves in current research and best practices to unpack meta-learning for everyone. Sonny's examples provide a real-world context to learning that is both relatable and accessible. *Learning in the Zone* is a gift to educators from page one. It will transform our schools and help us really dig into how learning occurs and how we can build meta-learners in our schools. Thank you, Sonny Magana, for the work that you do and for continuing to inspire us along the way!

—**Allison Staffin**, assistant principal, Cherry Hill West High School

Learning in the Zone really resonated with me. I gave the book the ultimate test by applying it to some new learning I was about to undertake. As the book recommended, I made a commitment to my personal mastery goal before starting the project. That commitment changed my attitude toward my learning. Then I imagined the reward for completing the journey, and I kept a learning journey journal to chronicle my emotional state, motivation, and progress toward my goal. What this did for me is exactly what it can do for our students—it made me hyperaware of my learning abilities and my progress. The feedback loop was within me, not a teacher. I became the author of my own learning adventure. This is like a superpower we can give our students as they become meta-learners. This is not a book to just read—it is a book to apply to your and your students' learning adventures.

—**Mike Morrison**, chief technology officer,
Laguna Beach Unified School District

This book had my full attention when I read the words, "Mastery is made manifest by our actions." *Learning in the Zone* masterfully tells a story of curiosity, skills, practice, self-reflection, and perseverance to meet one's self-imposed goals. Learning how to operationalize our habits is music to our ears (pun intended!). The seven habits of meta-learners run parallel to most of the common practices of a culturally responsive practitioner and key areas of social-emotional learning. The templates, sentence stems, and data points will allow teachers and students opportunities to grow to their fullest potential. As usual, Dr. Magana provides a resource that will allow the easiest access points to K–12 educators. This book is for us all.

—**Nyree Clark**, educator and curriculum program specialist,
Colton Joint Unified School District

I absolutely, positively LOVE this book! *Learning in the Zone* equips educators with high-impact strategies that make meaningful learning so effortless that it almost feels like cheating. Relying on research and cognitive science, Magana describes how to connect students with meta-learning habits that will prepare them for a lifetime of learning. Teachers will love how these meta-learning habits will keep their classrooms humming—and student achievement soaring!

—**Matt Miller**, educator, speaker, and
author of *Ditch That Textbook*

Teachers and leaders reignite their own love of teaching *and* learning by guiding their students into the learning zone. Sonny's quick wit, relevant examples, and humor provide a soulful master lesson on "tuning in" your students to lifelong learning through the seven meta-learning habits. *Learning in the Zone* will help you get your students off the bench and on the path to mastery in a thriving classroom.

—**Tom Charouhas**, educator,
Rosehill Junior High School

Dr. Magana provides us with a conceptual framework for meta-learning that can be used as a model for all learners. The meta-learning framework consists of seven habits that are illustrated through Dr. Magana's telling of his journey as a guitar player. This storytelling engages the reader and provides a detailed example of each habit in action. Dr. Magana grounds each habit in science and research. Each chapter includes useful strategies and tools to implement the seven habits in the classroom. Dr. Magana has done it again and provided educators with a valuable resource that will transform teaching and learning in the classroom for years to come.

—**Dr. Carla Taugher Aranda**, principal,
Pablo Tac Elementary School

A transformational vision and real path for learning. I cannot think of a time that this book was needed more. As we face a factious, ever-changing world, a new learning framework is needed to inspire learners to positively face the challenges ahead. Meta-learning is needed for our students, learners, and for ourselves to thrive in the world ahead. If you are looking for a future-forward process for positive change and true learning, my recommendation is to get in the learning zone!

—**Dr. Mike Chaix**, superintendent,
Rancho Cucamonga School District

One of the most coveted skills of the twenty-first century and the re-skilling revolution is the ability to create self-directed, creative problem solvers. This is achieved by the process of "learn, do, learn, do, rest, learn . . . repeat." As Dr. Magana describes in *Learning in the Zone*, every single one of us has the potential to experience optimal learning, the kind where our passions and abilities converge to elevate our performance well beyond our expectations. "Meta-learning" is the term he uses to describe the innate human capacity to learn how to optimize how one learns, unlearns, and relearns as needed and as informed by ever-changing circumstances. It's time to shift from "just-in-case learning" to "just-in-time learning." Meta-learning is the key process by which today's students become the wicked problem solvers of tomorrow.

—**Dr. Michael R. McCormick**, superintendent, Val Verde Unified School District

In *Learning in the Zone*, Dr. Sonny Magana introduces seven habits used by meta-learners. Educators need no longer wonder how to foster the "lifelong learner" so idealized in education. Dr. Magana has laid a yellow brick road for educators wishing to understand and move students into their optimal learning zone. Sonny shares his personal and relatable experience learning the guitar to illustrate how we, as educators, can recognize and develop masterful learners. Every student deserves transcendent learning experiences, and every teacher and leader needs this book to guide the way!

—**Marlena Hebern**, educator, coauthor of the EduProtocols Field Guides

Having a class full of motivated, independent, enthusiastic learners may be the dream of just about every classroom educator, no matter the learning level. Dr. Magana's *Learning in the Zone* presents a unique methodology informed by his own reflections on achieving mastery and fortified by key concepts from the learning sciences, metaphysics, philosophy, and biology. This system encompasses the whole learner and learning itself. Incorporating these meta-learning strategies into one's instruction can empower learners to find the motivation, resources, processes, and effort to achieve his or her learning goals and offers hope not only for the learner but for public education itself. As we've come to expect from Dr. Magana, he provides a friendly and usable framework to guide educators as they work to draw out the best in students and equip them for lifelong learning.

—**Dr. Steven B. Hickman**, coordinator, educational technology services, Riverside County Office of Education

Learning in the Zone is a book that every teacher and school leader should read. This book rightly places learners and their learning at the absolute heart of our attention and discussions. But more than that, it focuses on what learning feels like, how it is experienced, and what is happening inside the hearts and minds of us all as we learn. These are aspects that evidence shows make the difference between a successful year at school and a successful life as a fulfilled human being. In his typical highly skilled way, Sonny takes us on a powerful journey. He artfully weaves together firsthand experiences with key research from around the world. Importantly, he brings out practical strategies for us to reflect on, act upon, and embed within our own thinking and practices so that we might become better teachers, and so that our students might become successful lifelong learners. This is a must-read for all those working in education.

—**Dr. Fiona Aubrey-Smith**, educator, author, and director of One Life Learning

I love how Sonny's new book makes complex brain research so approachable to "regular teachers." When we ignore how the brain of the human child actually works, we tend to build dependency on authoritarian tropes and attempts to have students learn by force and coercion. I'm excited that Sonny continues to make his research findings both relatable and actionable. I hope educators will take the bait and maximize learning with elegance and grace for once and for all. It's long overdue. BRAVO, Sonny!

—**Jon Corippo**, educator, coauthor of the EduProtocols Field Guides

Learning in the Zone is a masterful explanation of our innate ability to learn. Dr. Magana's seven meta-learning habits ensure we have the cognitive tools we all need to become successful in life. *Learning in the Zone* is a beacon for educators and leaders guiding students to achieving their fullest potential.

—**Dr. Robert McCollum**, assistant superintendent, Hesperia Unified School District

The T3 Framework introduced by Sonny Magana in *Disruptive Classroom Technologies* provided much-needed in-depth guidance through which learning organizations may embrace a disruptive approach in technology use to achieve transcendence with teachers and students alike. That model was both actionable and visionary, leading learners and learning to a place of transcendence where inquiry design and social entrepreneurship seek to address twenty-first-century problems and opportunities. In his latest work, Sonny Magana takes us to another level—inside the individual and into the learning zone, where circumstances converge to produce that wonderful sense of mastery. Introducing us to meta-learning—the innate human capacity to learn how to optimize how one learns, unlearns, and relearns as needed and as informed by ever-changing circumstances—Sonny Magana once again "goes meta," rising above current conditions and showing us how the task at hand relates to our bigger picture. Whole-learner well-being and mastery are THE essential literacies for the twenty-first century and beyond.

—**Tom Finn**, CEO and employee co-owner, AVID Products, Inc.

In *Learning in the Zone*, Dr. Magana offers leaders, teachers, and students tangible strategies to achieve the seven habits of meta-learning, taking student-centered learning to new heights. The focus is on the learner gaining confidence to not only set personal mastery goals but to successfully achieve them while enjoying the process and envisioning the product. Skills such as self-regulation, determination, and reflection help learners connect to and invest in their studies, supporting a sense of student

agency that extends beyond the classroom. In addition, working to achieve these habits supports learners as they grow into avid lifelong learners, building confidence and revealing how their emotional state and cognitive growth work together in the process of achievement. Dr. Magana's anecdotes and examples help the reader envision this process and the product, and the connection to effective pedagogical strategies, such as EduProtocols and social and emotional learning practices, give educators the tools to support the habits of meta-learning with students of all ages.
—**Heather Esposito**, teacher, technology coach, Cherry Hill School District

Sonny has created another must-read. *Learning in the Zone* beautifully breaks down meta-learning and the seven meta-learning strategies. Not only are they well defined, but he also provides ways in which one can implement them immediately in both our personal lives as well as in classrooms. The reflections and resources are spot-on. He seamlessly mixes his experiences and ways for others to get started. Imagine a way to elevate your and your students' learning, but look no further—this is it!
—**Lisa M. Nowakowski**, educator, coauthor of *The EduProtocol Field Guide Math Edition*

In *Learning in the Zone*, Sonny Magana masterfully provides the road map for us to dramatically grow our learning power. The activities for each of the seven steps to meta-learning allow the reader to develop the necessary habits for deep and systematic learning. Dr. Magana seamlessly weaves both research and practice to explain the meta-learning framework. Moreover, Sonny provides clear direction for how educators can help their students become meta-learners. This is not only a compelling read; it is a guide for truly transformative learning that can be used for self-renewal.
—**Marcia Russell**, director of educator support and effectiveness, Ventura County Office of Education

I began teaching as a second career in my early thirties. Coming from a fast-paced, innovative high-tech company, I felt that there was something seriously wrong with the surface-level teaching I encountered as a new teacher. Unfortunately, there can be an alarming disconnect between pedagogy and lack of student achievement. As educators, we must remember that we are essentially brain scientists in the field of student learning. Dr. Sonny Magana's *Learning in the Zone* is filled with fascinating information and research about how the brain learns—from your emotional state to the balance of collective classroom contribution to learning goals. His seven habits of meta-learning are the prescription needed for today's educators to effectively prepare their students for tomorrow's world.

—**Jennifer Goodman**, educator, Hesperia Junior High School

Learning in the Zone really resonates with me. I appreciate the connection and references to the influence music had on Sonny's learning journey. I absolutely LOVE the connection to the emotions of learning as I don't think we talk about this enough in education, especially as it relates to adult learners. Learning has always been an emotional experience for me personally, and I appreciate the synthesis of effective habits, emotional intelligence, and perseverance this book provides to readers. I hope all educators read *Learning in the Zone*—not just for how they can help their students learn but also to rediscover their own love of learning.

—**Dr. Julie D. Judd, EdD,** chief technology officer, Ventura County Office of Education

Dr. Sonny Magana challenges us to take a "meta-moment" and consider what matters most as we continue to navigate complexity and change. Emotional self-regulation, as Sonny notes, is critical, as emotions are gatekeepers for motivation, attention, and cognition. *Learning in the Zone* is a compelling blend of neuroscience and practice explored through Sonny's personal reflection on learning how to learn, unlearn, and relearn.

—**Mark Sparvell**, education director, Microsoft

Learning in the Zone provides a much-needed framework to help leaders and teachers help students. Dr. Magana's seven meta-learning habits connects both the hearts and minds of our students in the mastery learning process. Dr. Magana shows us how school systems can shift from producing fact-memorizers to producing meta-learners who have a strong sense of agency and self-efficacy.

—**Faysel Bell**, principal, Hesperia Junior High School

I've been a big fan of Sonny's work for a long time. His new book, *Learning in the Zone*, introduces us to the fascinating world of meta-learning. I love that he takes complex research and breaks it down into practical things that any teacher or parent can do. Sonny makes it so easy to understand and develop the seven meta-learning habits that our students need to be successful in school and in life. After the chaos of COVID, meta-learning should be the new normal in schools.

—**Alice Keeler**, author of *50 Things You Can Do with Google Classroom*

LEARNING IN THE ZONE

DR. SONNY MAGANA

LEARNING IN THE ZONE

The 7 Habits of Meta-Learners

FOREWORD BY JOHN HATTIE

Learning in the Zone: The Seven Habits of Meta-Learners
© 2022 Sonny Magana

All rights reserved. No part of this publication may be reproduced in any form or by any electronic or mechanical means, including information storage and retrieval systems, without permission in writing by the publisher, except by a reviewer who may quote brief passages in a review. For information regarding permission, contact the publisher at books@daveburgessconsulting.com.

> This book is available at special discounts when purchased in quantity for educational purposes or for use as premiums, promotions, or fundraisers. For inquiries and details, contact the publisher at books@daveburgessconsulting.com.

Published by Dave Burgess Consulting, Inc.
San Diego, CA
DaveBurgessConsulting.com

Library of Congress Control Number: 2022940825
Paperback ISBN: 978-1-956306-29-3
Ebook ISBN: 978-1-956306-30-9

Cover and interior design by Liz Schreiter
Edited and produced by Reading List Editorial
ReadingListEditorial.com

*For Tracey: I can't do anything except
be in love with you.*

CONTENTS

Foreword 1
Preface 5

Chapter 1: What Is the Zone? 8
Chapter 2: Making Commitment a Habit 19
Chapter 3: Making a Habit of Self-Regulation 33
Chapter 4: Making a Habit of Leveraging Prior Knowledge . . 54
Chapter 5: Making a Habit of Contributive Learning 70
Chapter 6: Making a Habit of Using Learning Frameworks . . 84
Chapter 7: Making a Habit of Connecting, Categorizing,
 and Reflecting 100
Chapter 8: Making a Habit of Meta-Feedback 114
Chapter 9: All Together Now 127

References 136
Acknowledgments 139
About Dr. Sonny Magana 140
More from Dave Burgess Consulting, Inc. 142

FOREWORD

My latest passion is crosswords. On Sunday, I print the big four crossword puzzles (*New York Times*, *Los Angeles Times*, *Universal*, and—the best—Birnholz's *Washington Post*) and for a few hours am obsessed (according to my wife, Janet), engaged (according to my sons), and *in the zone* (according to me). I like bringing together the across and down clues, the theme answers, the cleverness of some clues, and the sheer joy of the aha moment when a seemingly tricky clue is discovered. I love it when I'm in the zone. Does completing crosswords make me a better person, a deeper learner, a wiser scholar? No—it is just the sheer fun of learning. It's no different from the way many teens consider their video games, avid sports fans their matches, teachers their passion for helping students learn. Those with passions love to dive deeply into them.

We recently analyzed the major learning notions that video game developers use and suggested that maybe educators need to be reminded that these notions can be co-opted back into schools. The irony is that these learning notions came from the psychology of learning. Game developers do not see motivation as something that has to be developed—it is and has always been there in each of us. Indeed, students have deep motivational resources, yet the key question is why should they spend it on this (schoolwork) rather than that (video games)?

Sonny Magana also knows the principles and ambitions of gamers and that when playing and learning their games, they get into the zone of optimal learning. These principles include: ensuring the involvement in the task is equally as rewarding, if not more so, than the goal; the thrill is in the challenge—not too hard, not too easy, not too boring; learners love to learn from failure; maximize feedback *now*; be curious, and curiouser; one learns to play the game in the midst of playing the game; make sure there is a story in which problems are embedded; learning can be emotional; it's fun to learn together; and, we can each work at our own pace—we can amble, trot, or gallop. These are reasons why I indulge in hours of crosswording and Sonny in guitar playing.

As noted in this book, learning and schooling can be two completely different things. But it doesn't have to be this way. Perhaps we need to adopt the Singapore education motto: "Teach less, learn more." Maybe if students saw teachers *learning* as they taught. The fundamental principle of Visible Learning is for teachers to "know thy impact" by learning about the impact of their actions, beliefs, and culture of the classroom on the learning lives of their students. Maybe (as happened during distance teaching during the pandemic) there needs to be less coverage and more depth, more teaching students to work alone and with peers, more release of responsibility by the teacher, and more teaching students to become their own teachers.

Magana introduces us to the concept of meta-learning. He implores us to help students learn how to remove the barriers that get in the way of optimal learning. We are born to learn. We are born to be motivated, we are born curious, and we crave predictability. Turns out the human brain is a great predictor of error. We learn from our mistakes. We thrive when we see errors as opportunities to learn and when we explore our errors with peers and learned others. Sonny argues that meta-learning can be attained, developed, and refined by anyone with time, practice, and ample feedback. Yes, we often need experts (e.g., teachers, peers, AI) to rise above our current knowledge to see bigger pictures, learn about learning for future encounters, and experience the emotions of discovery.

My crossword fanaticism leads to personal mastery goals; it engages my emotions, effort, and progress; it is a building block for future learning (I am now creating them and have been rejected by the best!). But it fails Magana's big seven principles in that it is not that social. I love that he speaks of learning habits and how hard it can be to break a habit. Often, I replace one habit with another. William James, my favorite psychology writer (I named my dog after him), argued that we want to develop habits in our students—not the habit of acquiring more and more facts (unless we want them to win pub quizzes or trivia games), but the habit of learning, of becoming a teacher so they can continue learning, and of attaining excellence. "Excellence, then, is not an act but a habit," as Aristotle wrote.

We know some of the barriers. For instance, cognitive load means that we can only hold four to six ideas in our mind at once, we cannot easily dual code, etc. Thus, we need to teach the skills of handling this load, which is the essence of learning. We need to overlearn some matters to devote our learning resources to new ideas, discoveries, and curious matters. We need to, as James claimed, "Lie in wait rather for the practical opportunities, be prompt to seize those as they pass, and thus at one operation get your pupils both to think, to feel, and to do. Preaching and talking too soon become an ineffectual bore."

But there is more than habit. There is self-regulation (the ability to learn), developing and enjoying feelings and emotions from the act of learning, and developing a greater sense of self-awareness and self-control. Magana claims that "It's through self-regulation that we attain and maintain even-keeled equanimity." He's right. Further, meta-learners understand that learning is an active team sport. Learning successfully in teams is not always easy in classes when too many think that simply putting students in groups will lead to collective wisdom. Yes, most students sit in groups, but they still work alone. However, there are critical skills to be learned in groups, such as turn taking, finding the confidence to contribute (and thus not become a social loafer), and discovering that a group can attain a better outcome than any individual (including me). Such collective efficacy is critical to develop in students, leading to creating tasks that require multiple interpretations and structure assessments for both individual contributions and teamwork.

Enjoy this story about Sonny's journey in learning to play the guitar. It brings so many of these ideas to reality for us. Sonny Magana has truly moved beyond campfires and beyond Chuck Berry to become the Eddie Van Halen of learning.

—John Hattie
Laureate professor, deputy dean of MGSE,
Director of the Melbourne Education Research Institute
Melbourne Graduate School of Education
University of Melbourne
Author, *Visible Learning*

PREFACE

The word "educate" is derived from the Latin *educere*: "To lead or draw out from within; to bring forth and develop latent potential." I've long believed that the purpose of education systems is not to simply maximize the amount of information students memorize but rather to ensure that all students have ample opportunities to realize their innate potential as meta-learners. This book is intended to provide students, parents, teachers, administrators, and educational leaders with a highly reliable pathway for helping learners develop seven specific habits for optimizing how they learn, unlearn, and relearn—to become meta-learners. The seven meta-learning strategies in this book are intended to honor the original intent of education by catalyzing students' innate love of limitless learning. It is our birthright.

As a former classroom teacher and building principal, I've had the honor of drawing out students' latent potential since 1983. I've also long believed that the best way to celebrate my own teaching journey is to amplify the voices of my students. I sent the draft manuscript of *Learning in the Zone* to one of my former students, Wendy Smith. I think Wendy's eloquent and powerful response makes the perfect preface to this book. I hope you do, too.

—Dr. Sonny Magana
Education Hill
Redmond, Washington

Sonny,

I had planned to email you back and let you know that I hoped to carve out some time next weekend to read your manuscript as my life is spinning with so many obligations currently, but as I opened it and took a look, I couldn't stop reading! First, I will note that I love the autobiographical format. I have always had trouble staying focused on reading that doesn't spark my interest or books that are not written in an engaging way (think textbooks or dry research journals), and I often had to read things twice in college. I feel like I can learn best when I am hearing someone's story in their own words, because I can visualize it better. Also, perhaps because it really happened, a real story resonates with me. I thoroughly enjoyed learning about your youth and guitar-playing inspirations and how that applies to your learning and teaching. I fondly remember you playing your guitar and singing to us at ACES Alternative High School!

In regard to my own educational experience at ACES, the things that stand out to me the most were (and remember I'm forty-three now, so I'm searching my memory!) the welcoming, supportive, communal, and nonjudgmental environment, which I think served to provide a positive learning platform. How does one truly learn without that! In our teen years, we are faced with so many social issues and personal changes that an absence of community creates barriers to learning. Engaging students does not mean having them memorize and regurgitate information, as you point out. Engagement is in hands-on learning, team collaboration, and self-motivation. I am 100 percent a hands-on learner. Some of my most vivid memories from ACES include following the Thayers on their journey to the North Pole during our Polar Project virtual field trip and the excitement and awe around that, looking at specimens through microscopes in your classroom, yoga breathing exercises before tests, and you singing and playing your guitar for us. We were a group of kids each with different challenges who all pulled together to support and accept one another because that is what our teachers modeled for us. (Meta-learning habits #1, #2, and #3.)

To be honest, I think that what I gained at ACES was less academic in nature, rather, it was a platform for me to gain the strength to move on to academic success. It was a foundational positive educational experience that helped me to access the intrinsic motivation I needed to go out into the workforce, obtain some skills, and ultimately make the leap to attend college. (Meta-learning habits #4, #5, and #6.)

Our life experiences shape who we become, and clearly ACES was an experience that assisted in propelling me toward the field of social work. In fact, my undergraduate internship was at an alternative middle/high school (I'm not sure if I told you that), which then led to my employment by Snohomish County, where I worked with runaway and probationary youth. (Meta-learning habit #7.)

Your ideas about classroom learning causing dependency, in regard to feedback from others as opposed to providing internal motivation, really resonates with me. That is very powerful and so accurate. As a parent, I am very concerned with the one-size-fits-all approach to education and grading. We need better ways. I am grateful that there are innovators such as you to find them.

Thank you for sharing this with me, Sonny. You are an inspiration to me always.

—Wendy Smith
ACES High, Class of 1995
Woodinville, Washington

1
WHAT IS THE ZONE?

By instructing students how to learn, unlearn, and relearn, a powerful new dimension can be added to education…Tomorrow's illiterate will not be the man who can't read; he will be the man who has not learned how to learn.

—Alvin Toffler

Have you ever been in the zone? Chances are you've had moments when you experienced the exhilaration of mastery in some activity or task that seemed effortless. You felt like you couldn't miss. You were firing on all cylinders. Everything clicked, and it felt fantastic. You were completely in the moment, feeling as if you could accomplish anything.

But being in the zone is a difficult thing to define, because it's so elusive and often fleeting, and its particulars are different for everyone. Perhaps the only commonality to being in the zone is this: You know it when you're in it. You know you're in the zone when circumstances converge to produce that wonderful sense of effortless mastery.

> Here is a thought experiment for you to try right now: Take a few moments and think about some knowledge, skill, or task that you have mastered to the point that you were in the zone—that happy state where you experienced fluid, near-effortless mastery. Now think about the pathway that got you to that point. What were the strategies that you used to attain that level of mastery? What were the habits that you developed along the way? How did it feel to be in your learning zone?
>
> You've just engaged in a meta-learning exercise.

Athletes often talk about being in the zone in the context of masterful athletic performance. Basketball hall of famer, Rhodes Scholar, and former United States senator Bill Bradley once played a game as a member of the New York Knicks during which, in a series of six blind turn-around jump shots—arguably one of the hardest shots in basketball—the ball hit nothing but net. He explained afterward that he was just in the zone. He felt like the basket was the size of a trash can, and he just couldn't miss. Michael Jordan's legendary thirty-eight-point game in the NBA Finals—during which he was sick with the flu—is a case study in zone-ness. The Great One, Wayne Gretzky, epitomized playing hockey in the zone. He seemed to be able to predict where the puck was going to be so that he could get to it before anyone else on the ice.

But the zone is not just applicable to athletic performance. Artists frequently describe sustained bursts of optimal performance where they are so focused in the creative process that time seems to stand still. Hours go by in what seem like minutes. Pablo Picasso would spend days working nonstop on one of his masterpieces in a state of creative ecstasy. Jack Kerouac reportedly wrote his classic *On the Road* in one single burst of nonstop creativity.

Masterful musicians describe experiencing transcendent moments when they are so focused on playing that they attain near-effortless perfection. Jimi Hendrix, Prince, and Stevie Ray Vaughn were virtuoso guitarists whose live performances exemplified zone-ness. Musicians also talk about being in the zone with different terms: "playing in the pocket" is a musical description of the zone that may have come from old analog recording machines that would literally etch a groove into vinyl discs. Playing in the pocket is the moment the groove is so deep that everyone in the band just gets sucked into it, staying right on the beat, listening intently, and playing off one another, completely in sync.

The examples above focus on performing in the zone once one has already gained a degree of mastery over the skill at hand. But what does it take for an athlete, musician, or learner to attain the knowledge and skills to make zone-ness possible? Is there such a thing as an optimal zone for learning itself? It turns out there is. Every single one of us has the potential to experience optimal learning, the kind where our passions and abilities converge to elevate our performance well beyond our expectations. This does not have to happen simply by chance. In fact, after researching this phenomenon for four decades, I am convinced that human beings can control when, where, and how long we experience optimal learning. It is simply a matter of monitoring seven different indicators that are highly correlated with optimal learning performance. These indicators can be thought of as easy-to-understand strategies that anyone can develop. If you commit to developing these strategies and use them regularly, then they will become new learning habits—what I call "meta-learning habits"—that can be implemented for learning anything.

SCHOOLING VS. (META-) LEARNING

From an early age I understood schooling and learning to be two completely different things. School was rote and tedious, but learning was fun. My feelings about school generally ranged between boredom, anxiety, and relief—whenever I successfully passed some test or examination. My classroom habits were based on the "cram and jam" game: the night before a test, I would cram as many facts as I could into my working memory and then quickly jam them onto some blue examination book the next day, hopefully before what I had memorized evaporated from my working memory. I got really good at cramming and jamming. But those habits were not aimed at acquiring deep conceptual understanding or transferring what I knew into different contexts. I was dispassionately exercising my short-term-memory systems to acquire and briefly retain superficial knowledge. That was the game of schooling that I had learned, and so I implicitly developed habits that allowed me to play by those rules. Nothing more or less.

But something entirely different happened when my favorite Beatles songs came on the radio. I found myself itching to play the guitar parts myself. I felt an exhilarating desire to learn that was a far cry from anything I'd experienced in school. I felt compelled to learn how to imitate my rock idols and reproduce their songs myself. My desire to learn the Beatles' music was stronger than the reluctance I felt about trying and failing. For the first time, I made a conscious commitment to learn something that was far out of my reach. That changed everything. Making the commitment to learning rock and roll music opened the door to a lifelong love of learning.

I experienced that learning how to play rock and roll music opened new doors to knowledge and self-expression that fit my identity. Teaching myself how to play the guitar seemed to be a natural process that was logical, sequential, and exciting. As I continued to teach myself guitar, something strange happened: I noticed that I wasn't just learning how to play music but I was *learning how to learn*. For example, I was becoming better able to focus on a challenging task for longer periods of time. I was also regulating the amount of effort I would exert. I saw a corresponding growth in my ability, which motivated me further.

The sounds coming from my guitar provided immediate feedback on how I was doing, but I was becoming more aware of another type of feedback in the form of self-talk. This self-talk was like an objective signal from an inner learning guide that cut through the noise of emotional uncertainty or performance anxiety. It motivated me and made me believe I could improve my performance all on my own. Anytime I messed up playing a challenging chord change, my inner guide would pipe up with a neutral thought that sounded something like, "Well, that's not right. What if you try it this way instead?" Then perhaps I would try a new finger or hand position to determine whether it improved my performance or not. This was very different from my schooling experience, because not only was I the source of the feedback, but the feedback loop was also closed in a matter of milliseconds rather than days or weeks.

My inner guide wasn't just a stern taskmaster that kept me disciplined about practicing regularly, although that was part of it. It was more like a watchful observer that rejected strategies that weren't working and transformed those that were into new learning habits. With time and ample practice, I began to implement these strategies a bit more automatically. Once these strategies became habits, I didn't have to think too much about doing them. I just did them without expending a whole lot of energy.

That was the tipping point for me. This revelation led to profound improvements in my entire learning life and sense of well-being. It seemed that teaching myself how to play the guitar transformed the way I thought about schooling. The experience gave me an entirely new way of perceiving that *the learning itself* was a form of literacy that I could develop and improve myself over time. I reasoned that if literacy is defined as competence or knowledge in a specific area, then why not consider becoming competent and knowledgeable about learning how to learn? I came to a greater understanding of *learning how to optimize my own learning*. I found my optimum learning zone.

WHAT IS META-LEARNING?

So, what is meta-learning? "Meta-learning" is the term I use to describe the innate human capacity to learn how to optimize how one learns, unlearns, and relearns as needed and informed by ever-changing circumstances. Meta-learning treats the process of learning how to optimize one's learning as a fundamental literacy. Taken at face value, a reasonable claim can be made that, like other literacies, meta-learning can be attained, developed, and refined with time, practice, and ample feedback.

"Going meta" means rising above or transcending current conditions to see how the action or task at hand relates to some bigger picture. It means being able to rapidly shift one's perspective from the tree to the forest. Many are familiar with the concept of metacognition, which is the process of thinking deeply and reflectively about how one thinks or how one has come to know what one knows. If metacognition is thinking deeply about one's thinking, then meta-learning is learning deeply about one's learning. It is logical then to consider meta-learning as the process of thinking and reflecting deeply about *how* one learns, in order to harness this higher-level consciousness to control the optimization of one's learning—to experience learning in the zone.

Finding one's learning zone is a function of developing and mastering seven specific meta-learning habits. Doing so will empower one in the process of becoming a highly agile learner who consistently achieves optimum learning performance.

THE SEVEN HABITS OF META-LEARNERS

Learning in the zone became my approach to learning everything. I was using these seven meta-learning habits so often that they became an intentional process. And it worked. Repeatedly. I began refining these habits and applying them to other pursuits and discovered that there was an immediate and positive impact, regardless of the content

I was learning. I found how to optimize my learning by being aware of these seven meta-learning habits and monitoring how strongly or poorly I was implementing them.

LEARNING IN THE ZONE

These seven meta-learning habits also completely changed the experience of schooling for me. Rather than dreading school, I actually looked forward to mastering new content I was learning there. I enthusiastically employed these seven habits when learning diverse pursuits such as high alpine mountaineering or earning advanced degrees. Meta-learning has also afforded me a sustainable form of self-discovery: I continually learn new things about myself through the process of meta-learning.

> **THE SEVEN META-LEARNING HABITS**
>
> 1. Meta-learners commit to personal mastery goals.
>
> 2. Meta-learners monitor and regulate their emotions, effort, and progress.
>
> 3. Meta-learners leverage past experiences as building blocks for current and future learning.
>
> 4. Meta-learners are highly social, active participants in contributive learning communities.
>
> 5. Meta-learners use conceptual frameworks to contextualize new learning content.
>
> 6. Meta-learners connect, categorize, and reflect upon new learning content.
>
> 7. Meta-learners are the source of their own meta-feedback loops.

Becoming a meta-learner made all the difference in the world for me personally, so I was compelled to contribute my newfound learning habits to the betterment of others. When I was twenty-one years old, I made the commitment to becoming a teacher and a researcher. Since then, these seven meta-learning habits have proven exceedingly useful to the learning processes of my students over the course of a teaching and researching career that has spanned four decades. Moreover, these habits are also strongly supported in the extant research literature about what works in education (Bransford et al. 2000; Bruner 1968; Hattie 2008; 2012; Magana and Marzano 2014; Marzano 2008; Marzano and Pickering 2012).

In my research work, I wanted to find out whether these seven meta-learning strategies were correlated with finding one's optimal learning zone and attaining effortless mastery. Recent breakthrough findings strongly suggest that developing these seven strategies are indeed correlated with an acceleration of learning performance (Haystead and Magana 2013; Magana and Marzano 2014; Magana 2016; 2017; 2019). These findings provide a road map to help learners develop the meta-learning habits that will unlock a limitless capacity for self-reflection, self-regulation, self-determination, and self-actualization. Such capacities will better prepare students not only for current learning challenges but for the uncertain learning challenges they will encounter in the future.

ORGANIZATION OF THIS BOOK

While learning each habit in sequence is helpful at first, the habits are also highly correlated and can be applied or adapted fluidly. As such, this book is organized into nine chapters: this introduction chapter, seven chapters that take a deeper dive into each of the seven meta-learning strategies in sequence, and a final chapter focused on putting it all together and exploring tools for evaluating impact. Each chapter includes research-based strategies for developing these habits as well as digital tools to help implement them in any learning environment. Each chapter also concludes with guiding questions and additional resources to use immediately in classrooms with students and extension questions to guide your exploration of your own optimal learning zone.

Chapter 2 examines the critical role that commitment plays in the process of finding one's learning zone. Without making a commitment to some personal mastery goal, there is absolutely no ownership in the learning process. The first step toward mastery is to commit to personal mastery goals.

Chapter 3 explores the importance of learning with our hearts as well as our heads. We actually feel our way through learning experiences more than we think our way through them. Learning in the zone is a function of not just learning about our emotions but learning how to master them through self-reflection, self-awareness, and self-regulation.

Chapter 4 identifies the critical role that past experience plays in our current and future learning. The knowledge base that we have acquired is the foundation upon which all new knowledge and understanding is constructed. We can find our learning zones by continuously tending to and strengthening our learning foundations.

Chapter 5 underscores the importance of social interaction and dialogue in the process of finding our zones. Learning is a team sport, not a solitary pursuit. We can more readily find our learning zones by identifying and building stronger bonds and communicating with our learning teammates.

Chapter 6 assesses the critically important role that context plays in the process of finding our optimum learning zones. Learning frameworks help us make sense of complex new information by putting that information into manageable and understandable pathways that illuminate the way forward.

Chapter 7 discusses how important it is to organize our learning into schemata, or mental structures, that help us categorize our learning. These categories need to be intentional, connected, and constantly reviewed in order to build our capacity for expanding our optimal learning zones.

Chapter 8 frames the remarkable impact that feedback has on finding our learning zones. The idea of reflecting upon our learning is familiar to most of us, but in order to optimize our learning, we must also master the habit of reflecting in the learning moment, as well as reflecting on that moment once it has passed. This chapter introduces a new reflection skill that I call "meta-feedback": sensing both the task at hand and the bigger picture simultaneously.

Chapter 9 brings it all home with a discussion on evaluating the effect of learning in the zone. This chapter includes research-based protocols and measurement tools that will help guide the development of optimal learning for all students. When schools shift from being places of mass memorization and regurgitation to optimal learning zones, the entire system will markedly change for the betterment of society.

2
MAKING COMMITMENT A HABIT

Until one is committed, there is hesitancy, the chance to draw back, always ineffectiveness. Concerning all acts of initiative and creation there is one elementary truth, the ignorance of which kills countless ideas and splendid plans: that the moment one definitely commits oneself, then Providence moves too.

—William Hutchison Murray

WHAT MAKES A HABIT A HABIT?

A habit is a procedure that develops over time to the point that it becomes part of our permanent selves. Habits are actions that we do with a high level of automaticity. They don't require a great deal of thought or consideration, but we don't exactly do them unconsciously, either. For example, think about learning how to drive a car with a stick shift. At first, the complexities of driving a stick in traffic take a great deal of thought and mental focus, but with practice over time, shifting through gears becomes a seamless set of actions that we do automatically without much thought.

All habits begin as learned strategies or procedures that are acquired through trial, error, and practice. Some are helpful and constructive, and others are not. Though the seven meta-learning habits are quite helpful for finding your optimal learning zone, each may feel awkward or uncomfortable at first. This is true for any new strategy or skill. But if a learner sticks with it and gets in ample time and practice, these habits will become a natural part of the process of optimal learning.

IMAGINE…AND COMMIT

In 1964 I first heard the sound of music that would forever change my life. My mom had a plastic transistor radio that she listened to while she cleaned our home. I was a hypercurious youngster, and I remember hearing a strange noise coming from the living room that demanded immediate attention. The sound of Petula Clark singing "Downtown" entranced me. I'd never heard anything like it before, but it was somehow already familiar. That's a testament to the power of musical hooks. I remember thinking to myself, "It's like sugar for my ears!" I knew I wanted more.

When the Beatles made their debut on the *Ed Sullivan Show*, they introduced a new generation of Americans to rock and roll music. The Beatles sealed the deal for me. The songs. The guitars. The haircuts. I was hooked. That plastic AM radio became my constant companion. I sang along with the Fab Four at the top of my lungs—much to the delight of my mom. Thanks to her and her transistor radio, the Beatles' music became the soundtrack to my formative years.

I was far more passionate about the Beatles than I was about schoolwork. In school I was a compliant—if uninspired—student. While I was proficient in my studies, I didn't really love learning in school. But in my spare time I found myself poring over every Beatles book, article, and fan magazine I could get my hands on. As the sixties progressed and the music got more experimental, I kept pace by studying the lyrics and the strange new sounds I heard on *Rubber Soul, Revolver,* and *Sgt. Pepper*. It seemed like the Beatles would produce a new album every year, each one filled with new and wondrous sounds. Sometimes, I would pick up my dad's guitar—a dusty old Sears and Roebuck Silvertone model—and, though it wasn't in tune and I had no idea what I was doing, I would pretend to play and sing along with Beatles records. It seemed so monumentally difficult to actually learn how to play.

After the band broke up in 1970, the Liverpool lads continued to compose, arguably, some of their greatest music. John Lennon's song "Imagine," an instant classic, was released in the fall of 1971. I loved everything about that song: the melody, the lyrics, the imagery. I was so deeply moved by its message of imagining "all the people living life in peace," that I was compelled to quit faking and learn how to play it. In that moment, I made my first commitment to mastery. It sounds funny now, but I actually *imagined* myself learning how to play "Imagine"! In my mind's eye, I saw myself performing and singing it to my mom. That was really all it took. That mental image was so strong that it compelled me into action. I purchased a cheap songbook and began to learn how to tune my father's old guitar and play that song.

As luck would have it, "Imagine" is played in the key of C, one of the most common keys for songwriting. So, I learned how to place my fingers on that distressed old fretboard to form a C chord. If I lifted my index finger, the chord was changed into the next chord, C-major-seventh. Then I learned how to contort my fingers in a more challenging way to play an F chord. At the beginning of one hot South Jersey summer, in my parents' backyard, I began piecing together the music and words to the first verse, "Imagine there's no heaven, it's easy if you try."

This was different from the learning that I'd experienced in school. My teachers would tell me what to memorize and, being a respectful and dutiful student, I would aspire to attain the goals they set for me. I was merely complying with someone else's wishes. I would also rely on them to inform me on my progress toward the learning goals. But when it came to learning how to play the guitar, I really wanted it, so I was the one who established my objective. It was all mine. I had clear criteria to determine my level of progress and a set of strategies, and I made a personal commitment to achieve my goal. But that wasn't enough; I also recommitted to my goal by making sure that I made the time to practice every single day. *I learned how to make a habit of making and keeping commitments to my own mastery goals.*

HOW DO I KEEP COMMITMENTS?

In the beginning of any learning process, there is always chaos. Nothing is in order. Little makes sense. New and unintelligible terms, information, and details whirl around our heads, making us dizzy with confusion. There is hesitancy, anxiety, even fear. There is also no clear way out of the swirling, chaotic mess. That all changes as soon as we make a commitment to mastering any difficult learning challenge. But you really have to want it. You have to believe it. You have to resolve that *nothing* is going to stop you!

A commitment is like a keepsake that we hold in our hearts. It's personal. But commitments will fade if we don't act on them. Like the old adage about writing, "One doesn't write, one rewrites," when it comes to commitment, one doesn't commit, one *recommits*. When we make and stick with our commitments, an extraordinary series of events begins to unfold that illuminates a clear pathway out of the chaos toward our optimal learning zone. At that moment, we resolve to summon the best of ourselves. That's when we take the first step toward our optimal learning zone.

It important to imagine ourselves reaching our goals and then to capture that vision. We are far more likely to stick with goals if we have a rich vision of what we want to achieve. What does achievement look like? Is there a clear picture of it? A helpful strategy is to first draw or sketch the outcomes that you desire. Beginning with the end in mind, sketch what you want to attain or what you'll do to celebrate achieving it. It's also important to connect a positive emotional aspect to goals and aspirations. For example, my love of rock and roll music motivated me to stick with my daily practice routine, especially when the going got tough. Anchoring our mastery goals in our emotional, literal, and visual neural networks offers a powerful combination that helps to add "stickiness" to the commitments we make.

When we commit to a personal mastery goal, we are not only able to see the end goal but to see ourselves successfully mastering something that is worth pursuing. Once we've made that commitment, nothing can stop us. This is something that has to be experienced, because the motivation comes from within, not from an external source. When it comes to making commitment to our mastery goals a habit, we're either all-in, or we're not in at all.

THE TWO-SIDED MIND

Making a commitment to a mastery learning goal nurtures our emotional minds. As famed Scottish mountaineer and author William Hutchison Murray (1951) put it, "Until one is committed there is hesitancy, the chance to draw back, always ineffectiveness. Concerning all acts of initiative (and creation), there is one elementary truth, the ignorance of which kills countless ideas and splendid plans: that the moment one definitely commits oneself, then Providence moves too." The very moment we set our hearts to some task, we experience the calm that comes with personal resolve. We summon our highest selves when we commit to mastering a difficult task to the best of our abilities. It also feels awesome.

That *feeling* is key to finding the optimal learning zone. Consider a simple metaphor: The human mind is a two-sided coin. On one side of that coin is the emotional or affective mind, and on the other side is the logical or cognitive mind. (Naturally, the human mind is far more complex than this simple model, but simple models can sometimes be useful.) The model of the mind as a coin with two sides helps to highlight that our emotional growth and development is equal to, if not greater than, our cognitive growth and development. It also underscores something all human beings have in common—that we are sentient beings who feel *and* think our way through life regardless of age, ethnicity, gender, or origin.

The fact that the human emotional mind is inextricable from the cognitive mind is absolutely fundamental, yet the emotional side of the learning coin has historically been given short shrift in schooling. High-stakes summative examinations have a singular focus on measuring students' cognitive abilities. While there is clearly a need to evaluate and measure cognitive capacities, much would be accomplished by evaluating our emotional capacity *along with* our cognitive capacity. Fortunately, the tide is turning toward whole-learner development, with significant increases in social-and-emotional learning (SEL) programs designed to raise awareness of our emotional minds.

This is strongly supported by research findings from such diverse areas of inquiry as evolutionary biology, developmental psychology, and learning science, cognitive science, and neuroscience (Benson 1975; 1987; Blackburn and Epel 2017; Breuning 2018; Goleman 1995; Harari 2015; Medina 2008). A straightforward interpretation of these findings suggests that human brains have evolved to rapidly process emotional signals to determine the threat level in any new situation. These emotional signals are really bio-chemical-electrical impulses that travel up and down our neural networks at blazing speeds. It seems that human brains are hardwired to assess the emotional security of any situation *before* any cognitive capacities are enacted. In the context of learning and school, how students *feel* about their learning supersedes how students *think* about their learning. Taken as a whole, these findings guide us to nurture the growth and development of learners' emotional minds as our first step in order to effectively support the growth and development of learners' cognitive minds.

We all have an internal emotional compass, and when we set it to an arduous challenge, it then becomes our own North Star, a guiding light that we can follow with full hearts. The challenge no longer feels so daunting. We no longer hesitate or doubt ourselves; we set our hearts toward conquering that challenge, and we go for it—full steam ahead, and damn the torpedoes. That is the point at which all sorts of previously unforeseen circumstances occur that help us achieve our mastery goals.

Making a commitment to a mastery learning goal also nurtures our cognitive minds. When we make a commitment in full knowledge of the struggle that we're about to experience, we actually build and strengthen new neural pathways in our brains. This has a direct and positive effect on the particular learning goal we are striving for, and it has a compounding effect on our learning *agency*—our belief that we can and will learn absolutely anything if we invest enough effort. When we build our own agency, our confidence about and capacity for learning grow exponentially. We're likely to establish even more challenging goals. In the process, we learn not only more about the content we're learning but more about how we learn and how to optimize our learning.

LEARNING STORIES

This is all fine theoretically, but the real magic happens in the *doing*. Mastery is made manifest by our actions. One highly effective way of developing the meta-learning habit of commitment is by using scaffolds that help guide and support our efforts. Scaffolds work like cognitive training wheels: at the start of a learning process we need lots of scaffolds, but over time we gradually remove them one by one until we're free of them. This section provides scaffolds that can be used to develop this first meta-learning habit.

When I made the commitment to learn how to play the song "Imagine," I imagined myself playing and singing that song for someone I dearly loved—my mom. I imagined playing the song for her in the correct timing, without making any mistakes, and without forgetting any of the words or tricky chord changes. The vision in my mind's eye of my mom's delight was so clear that once I committed to learning the song, I was compelled forward without hesitation. The process unfolded like a well-told story.

I've always loved adventure stories. These stories follow a classic sequence of three parts: a beginning, a middle, and an end. The beginning is the setup or the call to action, the middle is the conflict or the trials, and the end is the successful resolution and celebration. Finding our optimal learning zone is really about learning how to write our own learning adventure stories. We can find our optimal learning zones by imagining ourselves as the heroes of our own learning stories but with a twist—beginning with the end in mind.

LEARNING STORY SEQUENCE

Consider having students write their own learning adventure stories starring themselves as the hero. This process starts with students visualizing their personal mastery goal or what they will do to celebrate their attainment of mastery. This galvanizes students' resolve to committing and recommitting themselves to their personal mastery goals in ways that take them well beyond what they think they can do. Many of my former students would often feel surprised once they attained their mastery goals, but the experience sticks with them for the rest of their lives. The final step in the sequence is to actually celebrate the way the students first visualized upon the successful completion of their learning journeys. It feels great to celebrate our accomplishments, but it also builds confidence in our learning capacity and slingshots us toward the next learning challenge.

A healthy aspect of growing and developing as a human being is learning the strategy of delaying gratification until after the attainment of our goals. However, it's often tempting for students to celebrate *before* they attain their mastery goals. Giving in to this temptation robs students of important opportunities to learn how to delay their gratification. Repeated instances of giving in to this temptation will corrupt students' learning stories and may lead them to develop the habit of bargaining with themselves, or even "self-bribery," in which they exchange celebrating now for the promise of achieving something in the future. Those habits are far less constructive and effective and need to be unlearned, which takes more effort. Developing grit, perseverance, and self-determination is best done through experience. That's why it's important for learners to follow the sequence of committing to a challenge, struggling through the effort it takes to complete that challenge, and *then* celebrating success. Not only is it empowering—it fills students with a deep sense of contentment.

With each learning adventure students write, they strengthen their roles as the central characters of their own stories. They find and amplify their own voices, make their own choices, and develop their own senses of efficacy—that happy place where students understand that the capacity to nurture their emotional and cognitive minds is intrinsic. Over time, students realize that they can learn anything if they are fully committed.

DECLARATIVE AND PROCEDURAL MASTERY GOALS

It's also critically important to provide students with clear learning intentions and success criteria for all units of study (Marzano 2008). But those learning intentions and success criteria are not typically "owned" by the learner; they are most often owned by the teacher, the curriculum, or the textbook (Magana 2017). When students only follow someone else's goals and objectives, they become habituated to having someone establish goals that they then follow. This tends to build a habit of dependency, not capacity. Meta-learners have broken the habit of dependency and establish the habit of generating mastery goals of their own design. In order to develop the meta-learning habit of committing to our own personal mastery goals, we need to first learn how to produce and refine our own learning intentions and success criteria.

Personal mastery goals offer a powerful way to do this. These goals are learning intentions that are produced by students, for students, in students' own language of mastery. In order to be most helpful, personal mastery goals should be as unambiguous as possible. This helps students make a commitment to a clearly established vision—what attaining the mastery goal looks and sounds like.

There are two types of personal mastery goals that reflect the two different forms of knowledge representation: declarative mastery goals and procedural mastery goals. When a learner comes up with and commits to declarative mastery goals, they clarify the *conceptual understanding* they'll need to gain to attain personal mastery. For example, understanding the meaning of the Bill of Rights and understanding the similarities and differences between mitosis and meiosis are both examples of declarative knowledge. Declarative mastery goals reflect knowledge that is expressed through communication, using both linguistic and nonlinguistic representations—words, pictures, or both words and pictures together.

Procedural mastery goals, on the other hand, reflect procedural knowledge, or knowledge that is expressed by some action, strategy, or procedure. Being able to masterfully play a new song, solve for X, or balance a chemical equation are examples of procedural knowledge. When a learner comes up with and commits to procedural mastery goals, they clarify the *abilities needed* to masterfully complete a procedure or skill correctly, without errors or omissions.

So how can you help students put declarative and procedural mastery goals into action in the classroom? I have the great pleasure of working closely with Marlena Hebern and Jon Corippo, authors of the EduProtocols Field Guide series of books, who have developed a wonderful set of learning scaffolds called EduProtocols. EduProtocols are digital framing tools that guide learners through various aspects of learning, both individually and collectively. For example, in the Sketch and Tell EduProtocol, learners express themselves using the drawing and text tools in Google Workspace. Students first sketch an idea, concept, or process, then they use that drawing as a prompt to explain how they think about that idea or process. The magic happens when students see, read, and comment on each other's Sketch and Tell slides.

With permission from Marlena Hebern and Jon Corippo, I've repurposed Sketch and Tell to help learners develop the habit of designing and committing to personal mastery goals. It all starts by imagining the end of the story. Here's how it works: Have students think about a personal mastery goal that they want to commit to. It could be any type of mastery challenge—cognitive, emotional, physical, artistic, musical. If the mastery challenge reflects declarative knowledge, have the student write their personal mastery goal statement using this sentence stem as a guide:

> I commit to understanding _____ so that I can explain, model, and demonstrate my understanding without any errors or omissions.

If their personal mastery challenge reflects procedural knowledge, have students write their personal mastery goal commitment using this sentence stem as a guide:

> I commit to being able to _____ so that I can demonstrate, model, and communicate my mastery without any errors or omissions.

You or your students can use the Sketch and Tell template to draw and explain aspects of their personal mastery goals. The text box at the top of the Sketch and Tell template provides a spot for students to write down their personal mastery commitment. The sketch side of the page offers space to draw, using Google Workspace tools, what their personal mastery goal is, or even what they will do to celebrate their success when they attain mastery. On the tell side, students will use their own descriptive language to explain their sketches. Consider having students read and comment on each other's Sketch and Tell slides to promote the cross-pollination of ideas.

COMMITMENT MAKER SKETCH AND TELL

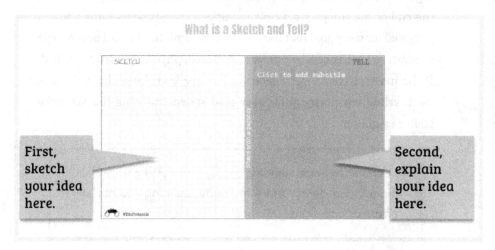

> You can use the QR code here to download a template that you can use to make a copy, save to your Google Drive, and share.

Use this tool to develop students' personal mastery goals strategies until you feel you it is no longer needed. With practice, the strategy of developing and committing to personal mastery goals and starting with the end in mind will become a meta-learning habit that will help students begin to find their optimal learning zones.

It might be helpful for you to do this yourself as well. Think of a difficult challenge that you want to master. It could be any type of challenge—physical, artistic, musical, cognitive, emotional, whatever. What is your personal mastery goal? What will it look like when you attain it? What will you do to celebrate?

Measuring Your Zone-ness

Evaluating the impact of new strategies is a powerful and sustainable practice that will help convert these strategies into personal learning habits. Consider using this scale to help students measure their zone-ness. This is a simple but highly effective three-point Likert scale that is commonly used in social science evaluative research methods. The three points are: 1. beginning, 2. developing, and 3. mastering.

THE ZONE-NESS SCALE

MASTERY SCORE	INDICATOR
3	Mastering: I am agilely and mindfully implementing this strategy to develop my "zone-ness."
2	Developing: I am close to agilely and mindfully implementing this strategy to develop my "zone-ness."
1	Beginning: I am committed to implementing this strategy to develop my "zone-ness."

Keep a meta-learning journal to help you track and monitor your implementation of each meta-learning strategy until they become habits. Consider combining sketches, diagrams, flowcharts, and narrative text.

Guiding Questions
Meta-Habit #1: Committing to Personal Mastery Goals

These guiding questions will help you gather your thoughts and develop your plan of action. Then, share these tools with your students so they can begin to measure their own zone-ness.

Regarding the habit of committing to personal mastery goals:

1. Where do you currently fall on the mastery scale?
2. Where do you want to be on the mastery scale?
3. What will you do to get there?
4. How will you know when you get there?
5. How will you express and represent this to others?

CONCLUSION

There is boldness and genius in making a personal commitment. It's like a clarion call to ourselves, summoning us to action. That's why making a habit of committing to our own personally designed mastery goals is the first step toward finding our optimal learning zones. The next step is to act in order to make the commitment a reality. In the next chapter, we'll explore the second meta-learning habit, regulating and marshaling our internal resources so that we get one step closer to finding our optimal learning zones.

3
MAKING A HABIT OF SELF-REGULATION

Through discipline comes freedom.

—Aristotle

BREATHING LESSONS

Before we begin, I'd like you to engage in a simple exercise that anyone can do. Please sit up straight, close your eyes, and take a few deep breaths focusing on your diaphragm—the large, dome-shaped muscle located below the lungs that controls respiration. You'll notice that your stomach expands with each inhalation and retracts with each exhalation. That's a good thing. This type of breathing is called diaphragmatic breathing or belly breathing. You'll inhale more oxygen when your lungs are more fully expanded through belly breathing.

Now I'd like you to take a series of deep breaths using a specific pattern: Inhale for the count of four, hold your breath for the count of four, then exhale for the count of six. Pause briefly and repeat. The pattern is important: in for four, hold for four, out for six. Now close your eyes and take a few minutes to find the ideal rhythm of your breath before you read the next section. (Open the QR code to access a guiding video on this breathing and relaxation exercise.) We'll return to this process a little later in the chapter.

STICKING WITH IT

John Lennon made playing music look like it was so easy—but it wasn't. I was excited about my commitment to learn how to play "Imagine" on my father's guitar, but I learned that the process was neither easy nor painless. The chord positions were quite a novel challenge at first. Contorting my fingers to form the shapes felt awkward and unnatural. They would often press against errant strings, causing an awful buzzing sound. I would also mistake one chord shape for another, which was tiresome. I made lots of errors. My emotional state would quickly drop into negative territory. But because I was committed, I gritted my teeth, redoubled my efforts, and stuck with it, even though I wasn't having much fun. My progress was very slow. It was also really easy to get distracted and stop playing. If I lost my focus and didn't practice for a few days, I lost ground. That wasn't good.

I decided that I would need a more effective approach if I really wanted to learn how to play the guitar. I started to get better about managing my time. I made a plan to organize my chores and my homework. I started spending less time goofing off with my friends, to make sure that I could practice every day for as long as necessary in order to achieve my personal goal. I hadn't fully wrapped my mind around it, but I was really beginning to practice the strategy of self-discipline.

The concept of self-discipline was new for me. In school, discipline was typically something that was imposed on me by my teachers or my coaches, not something I sought out myself. Even the term "discipline" had negative connotations associated with punishment—either disciplinary action for misbehavior or some forced activity, like running laps for being late to basketball practice. In fact, I had learned the habit of working to *avoid* discipline!

But this type of discipline was completely different. I was choosing to making time to work on something I was passionate about learning. I found that experience to be liberating. I learned that the discipline of establishing my own practice routine made me feel more comfortable and in control of both myself and, to some extent, my circumstances. Over that long summer it occurred to me that the simple discipline of practicing the guitar every day gave me a certain type of freedom—freedom from distractions that would keep me from realizing my personal goal.

Around that time, I watched a PBS special about an order of monks in Asia who could change their heart rate or raise their body temperature just by controlling their breath. I was fascinated watching these masters sitting cross-legged on the floor of a subfreezing cave with wet sheets draped over them. Within minutes, steam would begin to rise from their shoulders, and their handlers would remove the sheets, showing they had been completely dried by body heat! These holy men practiced a type of breath regulation they called *tummo*—or the "inner heat."

If they could endure such extremes, I wondered if breath control was something that I could do. I would imitate the monks by taking a few deep breaths to get myself focused. I'd then proceed to practice guitar for hours on end, often well into the evening. Whenever I wavered, I just stopped and began the breathing practice to gain a sense of calm. It was the first time I delayed my need for instant gratification. I was willingly investing my effort in the present for a more promising future. It felt like I was putting money into a personal bank account that would pay off in dividends someday.

Monitoring my own progress was also incredibly satisfying to me. I could see that it was taking less time and effort to form and switch between chords. When I increased my effort, my progress improved, and my emotional state began to return to the positive realm. I felt a unique sense of quiet resolve. By summer's end, I played and sang "Imagine" to my mom. I made it all the way through without any mistakes or leaving anything out. When I was finished, my mom clapped and hugged me, her eyes welling up with tears.

I'd never felt anything quite so fulfilling. Seeing something through to completion filled me with confidence as a learner. But the journey was somehow just as important to me as the destination. It was also fulfilling to learn how to regulate my emotions and my effort. I was surprised to experience a newfound sense of control over myself. I began to apply this new discipline in other areas of my learning life. I started applying a more disciplined approach to my science and math classes. I also became more disciplined as an athlete, lifting weights and running track. I started running cross-country in high school with a newfound can-do attitude. *I made a habit of monitoring and regulating my emotional state, my effort, and my progress toward my mastery goals.*

WHY LEARN SELF-REGULATION?

Though I previously regarded discipline as something that came from some external source, when I learned how to play the guitar, my perception of discipline evolved to include something that resided within myself. The self-discipline that came from within was far more enduring than the discipline I received externally.

The process of managing my feelings and effort on my musical journey led to a greater sense of self-awareness and self-control. A reasonable argument can be made that this is actually the goal of social and emotional learning (SEL): building and refining students' innate capacity to monitor, regulate, and exert more control over their emotional states. SEL is the means for developing self-awareness, self-determinism, and self-realization, but *self-regulation* is the destination. It's through self-regulation that we attain and maintain even-keeled equanimity—a state of relaxed alertness at which our highs are not too high and our lows are not too low. That's why self-regulation is the second meta-learning habit to develop in the quest to find our optimal learning zones.

Self-regulation belongs in modern schools and schooling. Too often, though, the process of schooling is overly concerned with cognitive rather than social and emotional development, partly because of the perceived difficulties of measuring things like contentment, happiness, and well-being. However, a large and growing body of research strongly suggests that well-being can indeed be explained, understood, observed, and measured by individuals and entire learning systems (Benson 1975; 1987; 2010; Breuning 2018; Csikszentmihalyi 1990; Goleman 1995).

NURTURING OUR EMOTIONAL AND COGNITIVE MINDS

The process of monitoring and regulating our feelings and effort nurtures our emotional minds. At the heart of finding our optimal learning zone is recognizing that we have control over both our self-concept and our sense of efficacy. While the human mind is the most elegantly complex organ in the known universe, it can also behave like a wanton child with a need to narrate all of its own experiences. So, what can we do to get our minds better behaved?

The breathing exercise I shared at the beginning of this chapter is an exercise in self-regulation that I recommend including in your classrooms and in your daily life. This practice nurtures the cognitive mind by shifting its focus from distracting external stimuli to the counting sequence. The rhythmic breathing exercise nurtures your emotional mind by quieting the brain's internal narrator, allowing you to focus on just your breathing in the present moment. Attaining and maintaining this state of relaxed alertness through breath regulation leads to tremendous benefits. Recent evidence strongly suggests that, at a cellular level, mindfulness practices like this have a profound impact on learning capacity, well-being—even health and longevity (Benson 2010; Blackburn and Epel 2017; Medina 2008).

The discipline of intentional breathing also nurtures the cognitive mind. It regulates a tiny but critically important structure in the human brain called the amygdala. Knowing how to regulate your amygdala plays a vital role in finding your optimal learning zone.

Here is another simple but useful model: Imagine that your brain is like Grand Central Station. The stationmaster controls the flow of trains rapidly coming and going from different destinations on a tight and controlled schedule. Instead of controlling the flow of trains and people, the amygdala is the stationmaster of your mind, a gatekeeper for the flow of oxygen, glucose, and neurochemicals to different parts of the brain.

When we feel uncertain, fearful, or anxious, our threat sensors send a warning signal to the amygdala. Like a good stationmaster, the amygdala immediately redirects the flow of oxygen and nutrients to a region in our brains known as the R-complex. The R-complex, sometimes referred to as the reptilian complex, is the oldest part of the human brain and is focused on ensuring our survival. When the R-complex receives a threat signal from the amygdala, it stimulates our adrenal glands and nervous systems to produce adrenaline and cortisol. This powerful neurochemical cocktail triggers an acute stress response that's known as the fight-or-flight response. Our breathing suddenly becomes quicker and shallower. Our temperature rises and our heart begins to race. This is because our remarkable brain is preparing our body to either fight or run away from the source of this stress. The fight-or-flight response blocks the flow of oxygen and glucose to our prefrontal cortex, which is the location of higher-order thinking and learning. With repeated exposure to stressful events, we start to experience chronic anxiety. That's not good. In addition to the obvious physical, mental, and emotional toll, this unhappy state starves our prefrontal cortex and significantly reduces our capacity for meta-learning.

However, recent breakthroughs in the fields of cognitive science, brain research, and positive psychology affirm what yogis have known for millennia: humans have the capacity to exert control over our amygdala through the discipline of diaphragmatic or yogic breath control. Clinical research evidence shows that deeply rhythmic, yogic breathing not only reduces the fight-or-flight response, but it also lowers our blood pressure, slows our heart rates, and reduces the level of cortisol in our brains. It also increases the amount of dissolved oxygen in our bloodstream. In fact, yogic breathing appears to gradually increase the levels of four brain chemicals associated with well-being and happiness: dopamine, serotonin, oxytocin, and endorphin (Benson 1975; 1987; 2010; Blackburn and Epel 2017).

REGULATING EMOTION, EFFORT, AND PROGRESS

A variety of evidence suggests that humans can assert greater control over their amygdala through the process of intentional, regulated breathing (Benson 1987; 2010; Blackburn and Epel 2017). I strongly recommend including daily focused-breathing exercises in schools as an integral part of SEL activities. Learning how to regulate breathing is a pathway for regulating both the emotional and cognitive minds. It's easy, free, and something that anyone can do, anywhere. Finding our optimal learning zone is a function of attaining and sustaining a state of relaxed alertness.

I've worked with a number of schools on integrating the practice of breath regulation with great effect. Each of these schools served a high-needs population of students who lived below the poverty line and were predominantly English language learners. Moreover, a large percentage of these students were considered "highly mobile" in that they moved their primary place of residence at least twice during the academic year. Within only a few months, these schools showed substantive gains in students' sense of self-control, their belief in their own ability to learn, and their sense of belonging within the school community (Magana 2016).

The research literature strongly suggests that feedback is not only critical to learning but that applying self-generated feedback for self-regulation leads to an explosion in learning capacity (Hattie 2008; Marzano 2007; Magana and Marzano 2014). Meta-learners make a habit of constantly monitoring and adjusting their emotions, effort, and progress through timely feedback loops that they generate.

According to the classical feedback theory, feedback is a continuous cycle that requires five things: a source, a signal, a processing system, an output source, and a feedback loop that returns the signal to the original source.

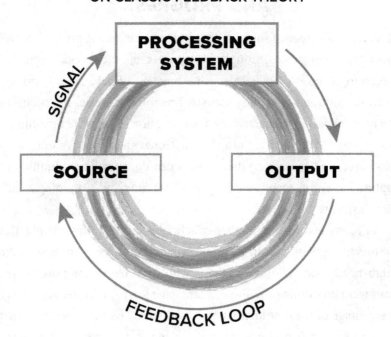

A MODEL OF SIGNAL GENERATION BASED ON CLASSIC FEEDBACK THEORY

Eminent educational researcher John Hattie (2008) asserts that improving the quality and quantity of learning feedback is perhaps the single most impactful strategy for optimizing learning performance. It's important to remember that Hattie's (2018) research indicates that the source of that learning feedback is *someone other than the learner*. However, learning feedback from an outside source has the potential to contain interpretive errors and biases. For example, there is an inverse relationship between subject-area expertise and empathy for novice mistakes. As an AP Biology teacher, I had greater subject-area expertise than my students, and as a result, I was disposed to harbor an implicit "expertise bias." Because I was so well versed in the subject area, it was challenging to understand or even empathize with novice errors or mistakes. That bias, implicit as it was, had the potential to influence the feedback that I gave my students.

External feedback signals—like summative and even formative assessment scores—often also reach learners days or weeks after the learning moment is over. Such "lagging" feedback is not nearly as useful for improving learning performance. That's not good. What is even worse is that if external feedback is the only type of learning feedback a learner receives, then he or she is far more likely to become habituated to having others inform their current and future learning performance.

Tracking student progress is, and should be, done by teachers who are trained to observe and measure student learning behaviors. But rather than learners waiting for teachers to inform them of their progress, I suggest that to attain their optimal learning zones, this process needs to be owned by learners. My science students really enjoyed the process of tracking their own progress and seeing for themselves the gains they were making. Not only is this highly empowering but there is a significant positive impact on learning performance when learners engage in strategies that enhance their ability for self-appraisal (Hattie 2008). Self-appraisal strategies help students clarify the learning intention and how far they are from that learning intention, and they help identify specific strategies to close that gap (Magana and Marzano 2014).

Meta-learners have learned how to unlearn the habit of external-feedback dependency by acquiring a habit of generating their own feedback loops to optimize their learning performance. Human brains are wired for survival. Since learning is a function of survival, one can argue that human learners are perfectly capable of generating their own feedback loops with coaching and guidance on how to best inform their progress toward their personal mastery goals. Finding our optimal learning zone is a function of generating just the right signal, from the right source, at the right time.

Attaining our optimal learning zone is really about improving how well we regulate three leading indicators of learning performance: our emotions, our effort, and our progress. These three leading indicators become self-generated "signals" that meta-learners monitor and track in continuous feedback loops. This takes the current feedback pattern that is commonly found in schools and flips it completely on its head. It also results in explosive learning capacity that is not only sustainable but seems to compound over time (Hattie 2008; Magana 2019). The students in my science classes also became quite sophisticated at tracking and monitoring their progress in their other classes. Developing the strategy of observing, tracking, and regulating our feelings, effort, and progress is intrinsically motivating. It's worth doing for its own sake.

HOW DOES ONE ENGAGE IN SELF-REGULATION?

The first step toward self-regulation is believing that we actually do have control over our emotions, the amount of effort we invest, and the progress that results from our efforts. Regulating our emotions, effort, and progress is a lot like adjusting the bass, midrange, and treble dials on a quality sound system. Students have the innate capacity to adjust their learning-zone dials to get the levels just right at each stage of their learning journeys.

The second step is to stop and reflect on the levels of our emotions, effort, and progress, and measure them using a simple three-point scale of good (3), fair (2), or poor (1). (This type of scale is commonly used in social science research to observe and quantify a range of complex, yet observable behaviors.) The language we use in a scale like this needs to be age appropriate and responsive to the learner. For example, using fewer words and more pictures works quite well with primary leaners.

The third step is to try a range of different regulatory strategies at different times to better adjust the levels of your emotions, effort, and progress. The focused-breathing exercise we practiced at the beginning of this chapter is a powerful go-to strategy to help regain our emotional balance and equanimity. The exercise of visualizing your celebration at the completion of your personal mastery goals is another powerful strategy. It's equally important that students get sufficient sleep, exercise, play, and proper nutrition as these elements have a profoundly positive impact on learning performance (Medina 2008). There is no known limit to the types or combinations of strategies that we can apply throughout our mastery learning journeys.

The key is to think of this whole process as a series of feedback loops in which we are the source of the signal. These three critical self-directed learning feedback loops will help you learn which combination of regulatory strategies works best for helping you attain your committed goals.

Even though the range of human feelings is quite wide, complicated, and variable, the act of stopping and observing our intrinsic emotive state gives pause to whatever emotion we are feeling. A single momentary reflection serves to lower the emotional "volume control" by uncoupling ourselves from emotional triggers. It allows us to focus on observing and quantifying that feeling, in the moment, and creates an opportunity for quickly implementing a regulatory strategy. For example, what is your emotional level right now? Are you at level 1 (poor)? If so, try implementing the breathing strategy to get to level 2 (fair). If you are at level 2, try implementing the breathing strategy coupled with recommitting yourself to your personal mastery goal to get to level 3 (good).

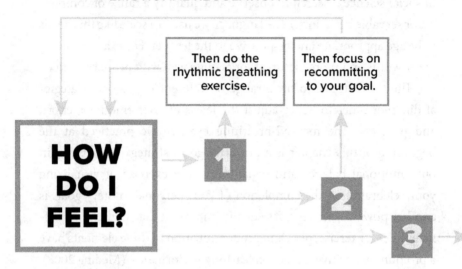

Moreover, there is an ancient five-step strategy for regulating emotional states that was developed within the disciplines associated with the ancient Taoist philosophy as described in the two-thousand-year-old book of poems called the *Tao Te Ching*. The four Taoist pillars of transcendent human experience are: simplicity, finding flow, letting go, and harmony (Laozi and Chan 1963). Another activity combines the diaphragmatic breathing strategy with an introspective analysis of one's emotions based on these four ancient principles. This is a highly effective way to help students more fully experience and learn about their emotional states, their triggers, and strategies designed to exert more self-regulatory control. With intentionality, this will help students to be more conscious about shifting their emotional state from level 1 (poor) to level 3 (good). The steps are as follows:

1. **Observe it:** Take the time to observe the emotion you are feeling in the moment.
2. **Recognize it:** Identify what this emotion is and label it.
3. **Own it:** Take full responsibility for having this feeling, as it is entirely your own.
4. **Experience it:** Fully consider the beginning, middle, and end of this emotion.
5. **Release it:** Let it go. Imagine the feeling drifting away from your present.

It's quite common for students to want to quit in the midst of a challenging learning experience. That's a great time to have students go through the following exercise. Have your students take a moment and reflect on the question, "How do you feel?" If they're at level 1 (poor), then have them try implementing the rhythmic breathing and five-step emotional-regulation strategy to get to level 2. If they are at level 2 (fair), then have them try implementing the breathing strategy coupled with visualizing themselves celebrating the realization of their learning goal.

EFFORT REGULATION FLOWCHART

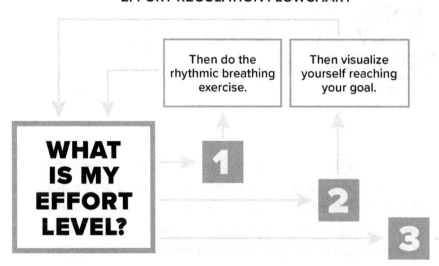

If students' feelings are at level 3 (good), then they can move forward to the next question: "What is my effort level right now?" This is a more precise way of asking how hard students are trying to achieve their mastery goals. Once again, breaking down the idea into three distinct levels helps provide guidance for richer self-reflection. For example, are they at level 1 (poor)? If so, have them try implementing the breathing strategy to get to level 2 (fair). If they are at level 2, ask them to try implementing the breathing strategy coupled with visualizing themselves realizing the goal to which they have committed in order to get to level 3 (good). Have students try using this powerful visualization strategy to inspire them to increase their effort to just the right level.

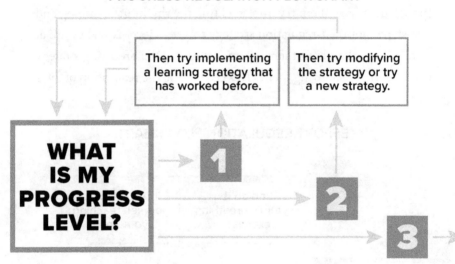

PROGRESS REGULATION FLOWCHART

If students are at effort level 3, guide them to ask themselves, "What is the progress that has resulted from regulating my emotions and my effort?" If they are at level 1, then they are just beginning their learning journey and are not yet able to demonstrate, communicate, and model understanding without any mistakes or omissions. What learning strategies could they apply to get to level 2? If they are at level

2, then they are getting close to fully demonstrating, communicating, and modeling their understanding without any errors or omissions. How could they modify the learning strategy they are using, or what new strategy could they apply to fill in the final gaps to get to level 3? If they are at level 3, then they can communicate, demonstrate, and model their understanding without making any critical mistakes or leaving anything out. *That's* when it's time to celebrate their mastery.

The final step is to learn how to apply the right strategy at the right time to move toward your committed goals. This takes time and ample opportunities to reflect upon the learning strategies. It's also really helpful for students to discuss and share the learning strategies they apply with their classmates. Once students realize that we have control over these three currencies of mastery, they can learn how to regulate them to find just the right levels—not too high, not too low, but just right. With time and disciplined practice, these strategies will become the powerful meta-learning habit of self-regulation.

THE MAGANA MASTERY TRACKER

The Magana Mastery Tracker is a free tool that can help scaffold or guide your students as they develop the strategy of self-regulation. Once again, this takes time, consistent practice, and lots of opportunities to discuss the goals and the strategies they use with their classmates. In time they will learn how to fine-tune the dials on these three leading indicators of mastery using the self-generated feedback they gain from using the Magana Mastery Tracker. This will help your students home in on their optimal learning zone.

MAGANA MASTERY TRACKER

Student	Teacher	Class	Date Started	Date Ended
Joey Ramone	Miss. Gradenko	Music Theory	July 1	July 7

Mastery Goal: I will be able to play "Eruption" all the way through with no mistakes or ommisions.

What I'll Do To Achieve Mastery: Chunking each secion, slowing tempo, reqular group and solo praclice

Progress Scale:	1 Not Yet Mastering	2 Nearing Mastery	3 Mastering
Effort Scale:	1 Not Yet Full Effort	2 Nearing Full Effort	3 Full Effort
Feelings Scale:	1 Not Yet Feeling Awesome	2 Nearing Feeling Awesome	3 Feeling Awesome

Date:	Progress	Effort:	Feelings	Reflections:
7/1	1	2	3	I'm not able to demonstrate this skill. I feel frustrated! :-(
7/2	2	2	1	YIKES! It's going to take a lot more work to master this! :-(
7/3	1	3	1	YIKES! It's going to take a lot more work to master this! :-(
7/4	2	3	1	I think I'm starting to understand but still have to work harder! :-/
7/5	2	3	2	I'm really working hard, but keep making the same mistakes! :-/
7/6	2.5	2	3	I'm understanding more and making fewer mistakes! :-)
7/7	3	1	3	I fully understand, can explain my thinking and am error free! :-)

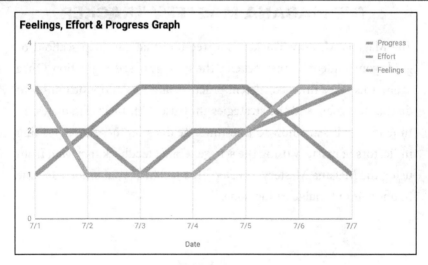

THE MAGANA PRIMARY TRACKER

Student	Teacher	Class	Date Started	Date Ended
Iggy Pop	Carlos Santana	Ukuelele	Mar. 1	Mar. 9

Mastery Goal: To play Twinkle Twinkle Little Star without any mistakes.
What I'll Do To Achieve Mastery: Practice 20 minutes every day.

	1	2	3
Progress:	👎	👎👍	👍
Effort:	🔔	🔔🔔	🔔🔔🔔
Feelings:	☹	😐	😄

Date:	Progress:	Effort:	Feelings	Reflections:
Monday	1	1	2	I have to practice my finger positions.
Tuesday	1	1	1	I think I can do this.
Wednesday	1	1	1	I have to work harder.
Thursday	2	3	1	I'm not getting better yet.
Friday	2	3	2	I'm starting to get better.
Monday	2	3	2	I'm getting a lot better!
Tuesday	3	3	2	
Wednesday	3	1	3	
Thursday	3	1	4	
Thursday				

Sentence starters:
- My progress was ____
- I tried _____
- I feel _____
- I know that I can _____
- Next time I will _____

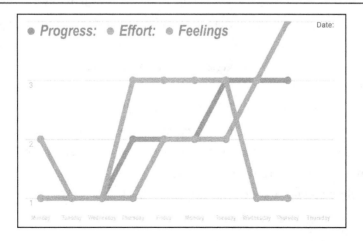

Have students fill in the fields with their basic details, their personal mastery goal, and what they plan to do to achieve their goal. Then notice the three scales: feelings, effort, and progress. Have students use the gray cells at the bottom of the spreadsheet to enter dates and their levels in the colored cells using 3 for high, 2 for medium, and 1 for low. Ask students to use the cells in the reflection column as a quick check-in to capture the aha moments they experience. There is also a Magana Primary Tracker with kid-friendly graphics that is better suited for primary-aged learners.

The Magana Mastery Tracker allows you to generate feedback loops to better monitor and control feelings, effort, and progress. The graph will display your unique learning story. You will also begin to notice a pattern that is common to meta-learners: When you first begin some mastery learning journey, your emotional state will start to drop into negative territory as you engage in deeper, more challenging learning. This is when it's easiest to become frustrated, anxious, or even angry. You'll notice that your feelings will drop to level 1. You'll be tempted to just quit and run away from the challenge. But if you learn to adjust your effort level by increasing it to a 3, you'll experience the freedom that comes from delaying your gratification. You'll be better able to stick with difficult learning tasks when the learning gets tough, and then your mastery celebration will feel that much sweeter.

You'll begin experiencing greater control over your own progress in new and powerful ways. You'll notice that your pathway toward mastering your personal challenge will become clearer and your goal will seem more obtainable. You'll feel hopeful that you'll reach your destination, and this will generate even more energy for you to invest in your journey.

Your amazing brain will sense your personal mastery goal getting nearer and nearer, and it will release ample amounts of dopamine to make you feel better about your progress and keep you on track (Breuning 2018). You're rocking out now, and it feels great. You will clearly benefit from experiencing the direct and causal relationship between your feelings and effort—over which you now have more control—and the rapid progress that you will make. The greater your effort, the greater your progress.

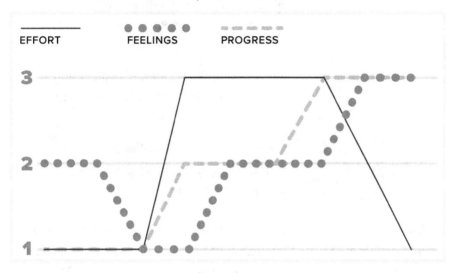

CAUSAL RELATIONSHIP BETWEEN FEELINGS, EFFORT, AND PROGRESS

As you make your final approach to mastery, you'll experience another amazing relationship: not only will you feel great, but you'll see that the amount of effort you expend will decrease *significantly*. This is a natural consequence of meta-learning: as you forge new neural learning pathways, it will take less and less effort to sustain your level of mastery. Seeing the relationships in the Magana Mastery Tracker graph provides a powerful feedback loop that will help you build and sustain a deep vocabulary of self-regulation strategies that work for you.

Measuring Your Zone-ness

THE ZONE-NESS SCALE

MASTERY SCORE	INDICATOR
3	Mastering: I am agilely and mindfully implementing this strategy to develop my "zone-ness."
2	Developing: I am close to agilely and mindfully implementing this strategy to develop my "zone-ness."
1	Beginning: I am committed to implementing this strategy to develop my "zone-ness."

Continue to use a meta-learning journal to help you track and monitor each meta-learning strategy until it becomes a habit. Consider combining sketches, diagrams, flowcharts, and narrative text. Use the guiding questions to help you gather your thoughts and commit to them in your plan of action.

Guiding Questions
Meta-Habit #2: Self-Regulation

Regarding the habit of self-regulation:

1. Where do you currently fall on the zone-ness scale?
2. Where do you want to be on the zone-ness scale?
3. What will you do to get there?
4. How will you know when you get there?
5. How will you express and represent this to others?

CONCLUSION

Developing the habit of self-regulation will take time, intentional practice, and clear feedback. It is also utterly empowering when we realize that we have control over our emotions, effort, and progress. With time and disciplined practice, these strategies will become a powerful meta-learning habit.

If through discipline comes freedom, as Aristotle taught us, then through self-regulation comes discipline. The meta-learning habit of self-regulation will become a springboard for you to develop the third meta-learning habit: leveraging past knowledge as building blocks for future learning. In the next chapter, we'll explore the why, what, and how of developing this habit in the search for your optimal learning zone.

4
MAKING A HABIT OF LEVERAGING PRIOR KNOWLEDGE

> *The self is not something ready-made, but something in continuous formation through choice of action.*
>
> —John Dewey

Nearly one hundred years ago, educational researcher and philosopher John Dewey taught us that we are all works in progress. We are in a continual state of *becoming,* which is rooted in the sum total of our experiences past and present. Dewey's principle of continuity states that all of our prior experiences are carried forward to exert influence on the present moment and on future experiences and decisions. The idea that our past learning experiences have an incontrovertible influence on our present and future learning may at first seem daunting or even dispiriting. This may be particularly so for disenfranchised or marginalized learners who lack extensive prior knowledge and experiences.

However, the research base that was built upon John Dewey's far-reaching work strongly suggests otherwise. The presence of caring, highly effective teachers coupled with learning environments that are conducive to learning optimization can have a powerful and lasting impact on students' lives (Hattie 2008; Haystead and Magana 2013; Magana and Marzano 2014; Marzano 2008). Humans are quite capable of making up for past deficits. We can turn those deficits into benefits by learning from them. The next key to finding your optimal learning zone is acquiring the habit of deeply reflecting upon and leveraging your past knowledge as a tool to solve current and future learning problems.

MAKING CONNECTIONS

Learning how to play "Imagine" helped me to become proficient at moving from a C chord to a C-major-seventh chord to an F chord to a G chord, then back to the C. I practiced this pattern so often that I developed a type of muscle memory in which my fingers could form these three chords with a pretty high level of automaticity. I could do it with my eyes closed. With time, and by varying how I practiced, I mastered these three foundational chords.

Next came a strange and delightful discovery: it turned out that there were lots of other songs I could play *using the same chords*, including what is perhaps the most popular song the Beatles ever covered: "Twist and Shout." I knew that song by heart, so I just had to learn the song's more up-tempo strumming pattern. Just like that, I added a second song to my repertoire.

This chord pattern triggered a musical memory from my past. Bits of a song kept rattling around in my head, its familiarity nagging at me, but I just couldn't quite put my finger on it. Then I heard the sound I was searching for on an oldies radio station: it was "La Bamba" by Ritchie Valens. To my surprise I found that song could be played using the exact same chords as "Imagine"—C, F, and G. The rhythm was different, so I had to learn a faster strumming pattern and that classic opening riff.

An interesting pattern started to emerge. So many of my favorite rock songs seemed to flow in a cycle or sequence of tones that I started thinking about as "rounds." I started organizing dozens of new songs from my favorite genre of music into the category of C-F-G rounds. Then I discovered something even more interesting: I could play entirely different songs if I reversed the round—starting at G, then going to F, then C, and then completing the round on the root G. I applied this new pattern and, just like that, learned how to play Steve Miller's "Take the Money and Run" and Bob Seger's classic, "Night Moves." I started taking note of the similarities and differences among the songs in the new category.

I learned new chords more quickly after learning how to play those first three. The chords seemed like building blocks that I could stack together to learn song rounds in different keys. New and more complex musical patterns began to emerge to my ears, eyes, and fingers. Over time, I learned how to play all the major and minor chords, and as my knowledge grew, my repertoire of songs also grew. I was building a base of knowledge that I could apply as leverage to learn chord structures and new songs. Intentionally strengthening my knowledge base accelerated my learning in unpredictable ways. Each time I learned a new chord, phrase, or song, I reflected upon how this new learning compared to what I already knew. The more I learned, the deeper my knowledge became, which in turn allowed me to learn new things faster.

I started keeping a song journal to capture all of the songs I could play. It was soon filled with dozens of songs that I could use as a reference guide. It was like the floodgates had opened up for me. I needed a way to organize my growing song list, and so I began categorizing the songs I learned based on their style: classic rock, Southern rock, folk, blues, country. This organizational schema helped me better understand and appreciate the specific tonal patterns within each category and between the categories. Each song I put in my song journal was like a learning springboard, launching me into learning something new about music in general and guitar playing in particular. Discovering how to develop and apply my sense of pattern awareness was a critical learning skill that allowed me to diversify into new genres of music that I could play by learning common patterns.

By now, I was off and running. I knew that I could play any chords, in any sequence, and I believed I could use this growing base of background knowledge to learn any song. It was just a matter of investing time and effort. My sense of self-efficacy, or my belief in my ability to learn songs, was developing at the same pace as my experiential knowledge base. *I made a habit of leveraging my past prior knowledge as building blocks for current and future learning.*

PATHWAYS OLD AND NEW

The capacity for limitless learning exists in all humans. This applies to every learner in every classroom, from grade school to corporate training centers. However, when consistently subjected to oppressive experiences that repress their extraordinary brains, some people develop the unfortunate habit of learned helplessness. This is an unnatural state of being that goes against our very identity as limitless learners. The good news is that if helplessness is a learned habit, then logically it is a habit that can be unlearned and replaced with new meta-learning habits. Finding our optimal learning zones is also about discarding old habits that no longer serve us in favor of new learning habits that do.

Reflecting upon the prior knowledge that we have acquired over time nurtures our emotional minds. Reviewing and applying patterns derived from previously acquired knowledge to solve new learning problems feels good. It's quite comforting to look back upon our past learning journeys and accomplishments. This practice builds one's sense of agency and the innate capacity for self-determinism. It also inspires us to attempt new, more challenging learning experiences.

Engaging in a cumulative review of our prior knowledge strengthens our knowledge base and, in the process, builds our self-esteem, our confidence, and our willingness to take cognitive risks (Bransford et al. 2000). Moreover, recent evidence from the cognitive sciences indicates that deeply reflecting upon our accumulated knowledge base is associated with the presence of dopamine, serotonin, and oxytocin—brain chemicals that give rise to feelings of contentment, security, confidence, and happiness (Breuning 2018).

Leveraging past knowledge as building blocks for all future knowledge clearly nurtures the cognitive mind. Our remarkable brains make *Homo sapiens* the apex learning organism in the known universe. Our brains have evolved to reinforce continuous reflection on learning as a natural function of our survival instinct. We are able to self-correct by continuously applying past knowledge to current circumstances in order to make necessary changes.

Engaging in cumulative content review in the classroom results in very high gains in student achievement and learning productivity (Magana & Marzano, 2014). This clearly nurtures the cognitive mind. This process is most often orchestrated by a teacher in preparation for a summative assessment or final examination. But learners engaging in their own cumulative reviews of prior learning can become an ongoing, powerful meta-learning habit that unlocks and sustains limitless learning capacity.

The adult human brain consists of about one hundred billion highly specialized cells called neurons. Each neuron is encased in a protective and highly conductive lining called the myelin sheath. Neurons end in structures that are called dendrites. If neurons are like the roots of a plant, then dendrites are like root hairs that branch off the main root structures. Dendrites link to dendrites from other neurons through connection points that are called synapses. These synaptic connections are like gateways that connect neurons in extraordinarily expansive and complex neural networks that make the London Underground rail system look simplistic. Biochemical and bio-electrical impulses travel up and down our neurons to dendrites in neural pathways. The speed at which these impulses travel appears to be affected by the conductivity and thickness of the myelin sheath. The thicker the sheath, the faster the impulse transmission. Some of these pathways are well worn. The myelin sheaths in these pathways have become thicker and more firmly established over time, increasing the transmission speed of our bio-electric impulses. Like an old friend, these established pathways feel familiar and comfortable.

Newer neural pathways are obviously weaker—at first. These networks are more tenuous and tend to have thinner myelin sheaths, which slows down the speed of impulse signals. That's why new skills we are learning or habits we are forming feel more awkward and uncomfortable. It also takes more energy to forge these pathways. But here's the deal: the habit of deeply reflecting upon past knowledge and considering how our accumulated knowledge relates to new knowledge thickens the myelin sheaths in existing neural networks and those in new neural networks as well. When it comes to learning how to learn, we literally make the path by walking on it.

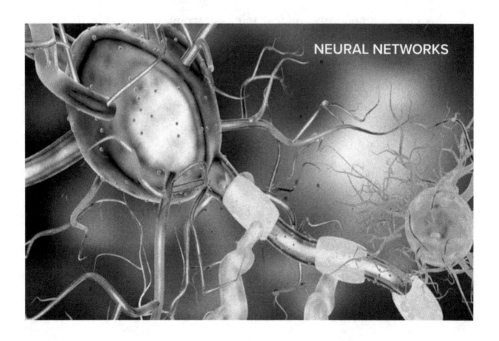

The complex brain-wide neural networks we have already constructed are quite literally the foundation for all new knowledge pathways. This has a positive and compounding impact on improving not only what we learn but *how we learn*. As it turns out, human learning is all about patterns.

PATTERNS HERE, THERE, AND EVERYWHERE

I first became aware of the importance of patterns when I discovered that there was a foundational pattern to my favorite rock and roll songs. It was like finding a hidden key that unlocked my latent musical potential. Becoming pattern literate accelerated my ability to identify a song's key signature in the first few notes, and it improved my improvisation during jams with my friends.

Nearly every rock and roll song adheres to a distinct sequence of three chords that is commonly known as the 1-4-5 progression. The first 1-4-5 pattern I learned was the C-F-G progression. Once I identified that the pattern existed within the song, I clarified the sequence so that I could more deeply understand it—learning, for example, that C is the root, or the first note of the C major scale. Finally, I was able to apply this new knowledge to expand my repertoire. This meta-learning habit of leveraging my past knowledge to acquire new knowledge gave me an enormous advantage in learning how to play songs and solos.

The three steps of identifying, clarifying, and applying patterns in rock music also helped me to categorize my favorite songs and styles into groupings based on their similarities and differences. I did this quite naturally. While there is great diversity in experience and background knowledge, this appears to be how the human brain works. The process of paying attention to new and emerging patterns and leveraging this awareness to learn new sequences or cause-and-effect relationships can been referred to as pattern literacy. Pattern literacy is the ability to transpose one's accumulated knowledge and understanding of prior learning patterns to new circumstances in order to bridge past and present learning more effectively and efficiently.

Human brains are hardwired to notice patterns and pattern disruptions as a function of survival. Here's a simple thought experiment: Archaeological evidence suggests that our hunting-and-gathering ancestors roamed the vast plains of Africa in a constant search for food while simultaneously avoiding being eaten themselves. The hominids who were able to successfully discern pattern differences between prey they sought and predators they sought to elude were able to pass down their genetic information to their progeny—us. The unsuccessful hominids, those who, for example, were unable to discern patterns that indicated a lurking saber-toothed tiger on the hunt, became what is generally known in the scientific community as...snacks.

The capacity to use prior knowledge as leverage for current and future learning hinges upon how well we are able to recognize, decipher, and apply patterns. An emerging body of research suggests that pattern "sense" is a capacity that exists with varying degrees in all humans (Bransford et al. 2000; Medina 2008; Hattie 2008). This research strongly suggests that the identification, clarification, and application of pattern literacy is one of our chief tools for learning anything. An even more important interpretation of this research suggests that pattern literacy can be nurtured and developed by every learner when they're given ample opportunities for explicitly learning, practicing, and applying it in learning environments.

The process of making sense of patterns begins with identifying a new pattern and determining its beginning, middle, and end. The second step is to compare the new pattern with an existing pattern in our prior knowledge base. This gives us a lens to better understand the similarities and differences that exist between new and prior patterning. The third step is to apply this comparative analysis to encode the new pattern into our permanent knowledge base.

The human brain thrives on the multisensory exploration of similarities and differences in the world around us. We look for familiarity in new patterns. This can be enhanced by deeply reflecting on the similarities and differences between existing patterns and new patterns. When we combine this reflection, which is a learned habit, with identifying the similarities and differences between past knowledge and newly acquired knowledge, our learning capacity expands explosively.

Pattern recognition is innate, and it's often done with a high level of automaticity; we do it, but not with a great deal of intentionality. This can be changed through the discipline of pattern literacy: purposefully seeking out patterns of increasing complexity, considering the implications of patterns, and then applying that new pattern awareness to solve new learning problems. The next section will introduce some tools to help you develop your pattern literacy.

TOOLS FOR LEVERAGING PRIOR KNOWLEDGE

Meta-learners use highly reliable sequence steps for leveraging prior knowledge in order to understand new knowledge or solve new learning problems. A very helpful strategy is to use a KND graphic organizer to help students arrange their sequence of learning tasks and strategies. KND stands for *know*, *need*, and *do*, as in: "What do I *know*, what do I *need* to know, and what will I *do*?" While you can create a KND organizer in many of the Google Workspace tools, this free version was created using Google Jamboard. You can scan the QR code to access the KND chart and then share it with your students.

The first step is to have students write the learning goal in the top field. For example, "I will understand and be able to explain the similarities and differences between metamorphic, igneous, and sedimentary rocks." Encourage students to be as specific as possible so that they can clarify their learning intention. Tell students that the more clearly their learning intention is written, the more helpful it will be to guide their learning tasks and strategies to complete those tasks.

KND CHART IN JAMBOARD

My Learning Goal:		
What Do I KNOW?	What Do I NEED to KNOW?	What Do I Need to DO?

The second step in the sequence is to have students activate and recall the prior knowledge that they can use to solve the current learning problem. Have students use Jamboard's "sticky notes" tool to brainstorm and capture everything they currently know about the learning intention or problem. Have students include as many prior facts as possible on the Jamboard—the details and ideas that they currently know that may relate to what they need to know. These are the basic rudiments of knowledge and thought that they are recalling from their knowledge base. Don't worry about having them organize it just yet; simply have students add as many details as they can to the KND Jamboard.

The third step is to have students to use their imaginations to think about learning strategies that they could employ to learn the items in the "What Do I Need to Know" column. This is the step that asks students to not only think about learning strategies they have used successfully before, but also to consider new learning strategies. Ask students to share the strategies they have used to successfully memorize new knowledge. For example, have they used rhyming strategies or songs to help them remember key vocabulary, facts, and ideas? Have they tried "storifying" new knowledge by sequencing knowledge chunks into a story with a beginning, a middle, and an end? Have they tried using visual strategies like sketching, drawing, or making diagrams to connect their prior knowledge with new content? Students can complete this activity alone, in pairs, or in groups, depending on their age and developmental needs. For primary learners, this type of activity might best be done as a whole-group exercise with the teacher facilitating the experience and capturing students' ideas.

The key idea is to help students get in the practice of framing new learning problems by activating and retrieving their prior knowledge. Once students have their prior knowledge represented as sticky notes, it will become easier for them to see how their prior knowledge relates to the new knowledge they need to acquire. To help better illuminate the problem at hand, assign different colors of sticky notes to each category, such as green for what they already know, blue for what they need to know, and red for tasks or strategies they need to do to achieve their learning goal.

This is a variation of the cognitive process known as chunking and scaffolding, where students take seemingly disconnected facts and strategies and then organize them into sequences. The connections they make at this point are critically important, so give your students ample time to brainstorm with one another.

It's important that students deeply reflect upon and analyze their prior knowledge. Anyone can do this using one of the most powerful analytical-cognitive tools available—looking for patterns based on similarities and differences. Ask students if they can find any similarities and differences between the sticky notes within each category of the KND chart. What are the common characteristics? What are the differences? What patterns seem to be emerging within each category? Then ask students to look for similarities and differences *between the categories*. What larger patterns seem to be emerging between the categories? How are the categories similar to each other? How are they different?

COMPLETED KND CHART IN JAMBOARD

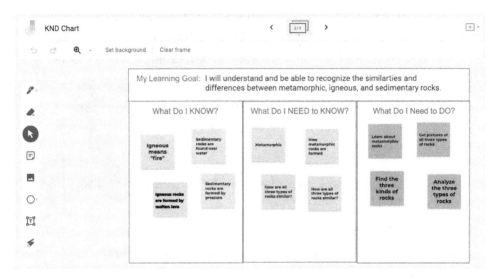

Consider using these sentence stems to help guide students through the process of exploring patterns based on similarities and differences.

> "_____ and _____ are alike because they both _____."
> Or,
> "_____ and _____ are not alike because _____ is _____, but _____ is _____."

Helping students to leverage their prior knowledge by looking for patterns will help them better frame current and future learning problems. Identifying similarities and differences is a critical cognitive strategy that students can use to make sense of new knowledge they don't yet understand. By implementing this learning strategy using digital tools, students will trigger their executive brain functioning. This is the higher-order cognitive system that students use to activate, retrieve, and leverage prior knowledge. Over time and with ample practice, this will develop their inferential reasoning system (Magana and Marzano 2014). This is the cognitive system that humans use to make claims, assertions, elaborations, and predictions that build logical connections between what we know and what we want to know. Consider using these if-then statements to help students make logical inferences:

> "If _____ is true, then _____ must also be true."
>
> Or,
>
> "If _____ and _____ are true, then _____ must also be true."
>
> Conversely,
>
> "If _____ is not true, then _____ must also be false."
>
> "If _____ and _____ are not true, then _____ must also be false."

You can also have students elaborate upon and extend these connections by creating analogic statements such as,

> "_____ are (is) to _____ as _____ are (is) to _____."

For example, "Feathers are to bird as scales are to reptiles," or "Glucose is to humans as gasoline is to cars."

For younger learners, consider using visual analogies that use pictures instead of words. You can do this activity as a "bell ringer" at the beginning of class or as an "exit ticket" to help students reflect on their learning experiences (Magana and Marzano 2014). This process quite literally strengthens existing neural networks while building connections to new neural networks. It's also easy, fast, and fun.

VISUAL ANALOGIES

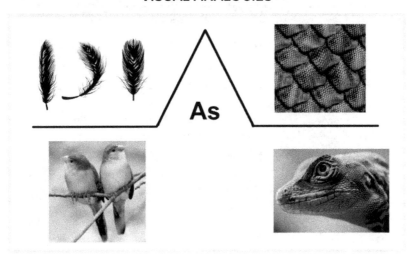

The final step is to continuously seek evidence to support students' speculations, thought experiments, and connections between prior and new knowledge. Ask students to offer evidence to support their claims using their past experiences or reliable sources of information. This can be done individually, in pairs, or in small groups. For primary learners, it might be best to engage in a whole-class discussion to affirm the validity and reliability of the evidence for claims. When students engage in this process, new neural pathways will emerge, improving both how they solve new learning problems and how they learn to optimize their own learning.

Measuring Your Zone-ness

THE ZONE-NESS SCALE

MASTERY SCORE	INDICATOR
3	Mastering: I am agilely and mindfully implementing this strategy to develop my "zone-ness."
2	Developing: I am close to agilely and mindfully implementing this strategy to develop my "zone-ness."
1	Beginning: I am committed to implementing this strategy to develop my "zone-ness."

Guiding Questions
Meta-Habit #3: Leveraging Prior Knowledge

Regarding the habit of leveraging prior knowledge:

1. Where do you currently fall on the zone-ness scale?
2. Where do you want to be on the zone-ness scale?
3. What will you do to get there?
4. How will you know when you get there?
5. How will you express and represent this to others?

CONCLUSION

John Dewey taught us that, like a river, knowledge flows from the past to exert an indelible influence on present and future learning. Simply raising our awareness of this knowledge flow nurtures our emotional and cognitive minds. It also allows us to learn more about ourselves by deeply reflecting upon what and how we learn and, more importantly, how we can optimize that learning. The more we engage in the habit of reviewing and building upon our cumulative knowledge, the more effectively and efficiently we are able to acquire and consolidate new knowledge. Like building bridges from prior knowledge to the present and future, the meta-habit of continuously leveraging our foundational knowledge as a tool to forge new neural pathways expands our limitless learning capacity.

Dewey's findings led him to assert that learning is a participatory sport; you have to get off the bench of passive consumption and get active in the game of optimizing your own learning. The evidence that I've collected over the past four decades corroborates that learning is also a team sport. We simply learn better together than we do alone. In the next chapter, we'll explore the next meta-learning habit of developing contributive learning communities that help us deepen and expand our optimal learning zones collectively.

5
MAKING A HABIT OF CONTRIBUTIVE LEARNING

The central motivation of all humans is to belong and be accepted by others.

—Rudolf Dreikurs

Meta-learners understand that learning is an active sport. They also recognize and celebrate the fact that optimal learning is an active *team* sport. We learn better together than we do in isolation. If the central motivation of all humans is to belong and be accepted by others, then finding our optimal learning zone is a function of how well we are able to share our perspectives and knowledge bases in contributive learning groups.

PLAYS WELL WITH OTHERS

I first experienced the power of contributive learning when I joined my first rock and roll band.

In high school I carried my guitar with me almost everywhere I went. I played it inside, outside, or on the back stoop. I played it in a tree. I played for my neighbors in front of my house. I played around any campfire I could find. While I was now playing dozens of songs on my own, something was still missing. Like every up-and-coming guitarist at the time, I had a deep desire to follow in the footsteps of John, Paul, George, and Ringo. I wanted to join a group.

In the fall of my junior year, I decided to take a risk and bring my guitar to school—something I hadn't done before. Almost immediately, I connected with other budding guitarists. We were all in various stages of development, but as I seemed to be a bit ahead of the curve, they all really wanted to learn *from me*. That was a first. We were all learning the same chords so we could play the same songs. Soon the other kids began bringing their guitars to school. We quickly formed our own little club that would meet whenever we could. During our lunch break and after school, we filled the halls with the sounds of the Beatles, the Rolling Stones, the Eagles, and America. Although we had different skill levels, we were united by our common goal: to play rock and roll music.

Until that point, my high school experience consisted of trying to get noticed by the popular kids. It seems silly now, but I was laboring under the misapprehension that I would receive some kind of formal invitation to be one of the cool kids. That never happened. Though I wanted very much to belong, I still felt like an outsider. But unlike the typical high school clique, our little guitar group thrived on inclusivity. We were a motley crew, comprised of nerds (like me), jocks, loners, burnouts, marching band members, and National Honor Society inductees. Our differences didn't matter—we taught one another new chords, songs, and styles of playing. Learning from and teaching one another was a newfound joy. I couldn't wait to go to school each day so that I could share, learn, and jam.

My classmates brought all sorts of amazing instruments out of dusty closets and attics that year. A wide variety of acoustic guitars that once belonged to parents, uncles, and even grandfathers found their way into our circle. Each instrument had a unique story, and we were amazed at the unique tones each guitar produced. Sadly, every guitar that had been put into storage also represented someone who had once dreamed of playing music abandoning that dream, along with the guitar. Our band of guitarists was committed to ensuring that didn't happen to us.

Learning to play music wasn't effortless, but it was a lot of fun. It also didn't jive with my conception of learning at school. Unlike typical classrooms in which learning is perceived as a competition for the highest grade, the members of our guitar group willingly contributed to everyone in the group. Every single person wanted to help me become a better guitarist. It was quite natural for me to reciprocate and help others who weren't as advanced. I found that I was a patient teacher and discovered, to my utter shock, that teaching someone what I knew improved my own playing significantly. My guitar pals and I were part of a larger collective, all invested in one another's musical mastery and well-being. Compared to what was happening in the classroom, I was learning more content and mastering new skills better and faster in—and because of—the group. *I made habit of becoming a valued member of a group of contributive learners.*

LEARNING TOGETHER FEELS BETTER

Research in the field of positive psychology (the branch of human psychology that explores the positive aspects of human development and the maximization of potential) strongly suggests that humans have a deep and abiding desire to belong. Ours is a species that has evolved to survive in unforgivingly harsh environments, due in large part to our tendency to form contributive groups. All humans strive to be valued, contributing members of some type of social cohort, whether a club, team, church, or learning group in a classroom. When it comes to optimizing our learning, humans learn better together than alone.

Engaging in contributive learning nurtures the emotional mind. We are sentient beings who feel and think our way through our experiences. Forming our little guitar club to help everyone in the club progress as musicians nurtured our collective emotional mind. We all wanted to be there to provide something of value to each other and to in turn receive the value of fellowship, comradery, and collective learning and growth. There was no one among us who knew so little that they couldn't teach something of value to someone else. And there was no one among us who knew so much that they couldn't learn something of value from anyone else. And all that learning happened quite naturally.

Humans interpret new learning through the lens of our individual background knowledge. While that's good to know, it's important to consider that the knowledge base available to any one of us is limited to a sample size of just one—and let's face it: one is the loneliest number. It's even more important to consider that one's individual knowledge base is potentially weakened by the presence of implicit errors and biases. This limits our ability to wield prior knowledge as an effective lever to fully understand and solve new learning problems.

Contributive learning also nurtures our cognitive minds. Expanding our learning sample size by becoming members of contributive learning groups is just like joining a band of diverse musicians. It expands and deepens the available background knowledge that can be brought to bear on any learning situation. It also serves to benefit the entire group. If learning collaboratively feels much better than learning individually, then learning contributively feels even better.

WHAT IS CONTRIBUTIVE LEARNING THEORY?

There is a distinct bias in our educational systems that privileges competition. Most learning environments are highly competitive spaces where students compete with one another for the highest grade or position in the class. Educational systems then rank students, teachers, and schools based on outcomes of classroom assessments and, more likely, high-stakes, low-value summative examinations. This competition bias imbues and impacts nearly everything within educational systems, from curriculum selection to instructional methodology and assessment strategies. What suffers under the yoke of competition bias is the individual and collective well-being of students, faculty, leadership, and their families. It does not have to be this way.

The Russian educator and philosopher Lev Vygotsky (1978) brilliantly explained that humans are social beings who make sense of the world around them by applying the tools of language and interaction with other humans. Vygotsky's constructivist learning theory, also called constructivism, indicates that the phenomenon of learning and experience is clearly and measurably enhanced through dialogue coupled with the precise application of learning scaffolds, or guides (Vygotsky 1978). We literally construct new knowledge by our discussions with more knowledgeable people, teachers, and tutors, whose service helps us navigate the choppy waters of new learning experiences.

We now live in a far different world than Vygotsky could have possibly imagined. The nearly ubiquitous presence of open-ended digital production technologies—from HyperDocs, blogs, and wikis to the wide range of social media—offers an entirely new and unique set of collective learning possibilities and affordances. That's why, for the past forty years, I've been developing a new learning theory that brings into consideration the digital age in which we live, learn, and work. I've decided to call this new idea contributive learning theory—or, contributive learning.

Contributive learning builds upon two widely implemented learning concepts: cooperative learning and collaborative learning. Cooperative learning suggests that learners divide work into individual tasks to cooperatively meet a learning goal. Learners initially meet to discuss how to delegate the tasks, but then they complete each assigned task independently rather than together. Collaborative learning suggests that students work together on each aspect of a learning task, which requires a higher level of communication and interaction. Contributive learning takes this one step further by shifting the focus from competing for grades and toward making valuable contributions to the group. Such a shift is likely to create a culture of learning that is conducive to generating collective student efficacy.

Contributive learning is rooted in the timeless idea that humans thrive when the focus shifts from competition with a lone winner toward collective mastery and well-being. There are three pillars to contributive learning:

- Emotion conditions motivation.
- Motivation conditions cognition.
- Cognition conditions contribution.

EMOTION CONDITIONS MOTIVATION. Emotional regulation is the primary driver for contributive learning. We learn best when we feel positive about our teachers, our classmates, our learning environments, and our capacity to learn anything. Ensuring that the classroom learning environment is welcoming goes a long way toward helping students feel like valued, contributing members of the class (Magana 2017). Have students use the breathing exercise from the previous chapter to reflect upon their current emotional state and to get to at least a neutral state—and hopefully a positive one. Shifting from a negative or neutral emotional valence toward a positive valence feels good. That feeling generates the motivational energy we need to tackle a challenging learning task. This is quite literally how to define the term "engagement": the investment of discretionary energy to a complex learning task. Simply put, the better we feel, the greater our motivation to learn.

MOTIVATION CONDITIONS COGNITION. Motivation is the secondary driver of contributive learning. Only once we've acquired ample motivation do we have sufficient energy to explore cognitively complex learning spaces. This simply takes a lot out of us, and if we don't have the energy to persevere, we succumb to ever-present distractions or the temptation to quit. When the going gets tough, only the highly motivated have the emotional and psychological wherewithal to stick with it and engage in heavy cognitive lifting.

COGNITION CONDITIONS CONTRIBUTION. The final driver of contributive learning is our innate desire to belong by becoming a valued, contributing member of a social group. The very act of conquering learning challenges compels us to share our learning for the benefit of others and, over time and compounding experience, to apply our knowledge to the betterment of society. It's a relatively simple algorithm: The more we learn, the more we learn to love learning. The more we love learning, the more likely we are to share our learning joys with others in such a way that contributes to the well-being and mastery of *all*.

Have you ever experienced contributive learning in action? How did you feel about the process of contributing to the learning of others and having others contribute to your learning? What was the impact of contributive learning on the quality and quantity of your learning?

HOW DO YOU DEVELOP CONTRIBUTIVE LEARNING GROUPS?

John Dewey (1938) taught us that learning is a participatory sport—you have to get off the bench and get in the game. My experience and research guide me to believe that not only is optimal learning an active experience, but it is also a collective experience. We learn better together as a team than as individuals (Magana 2019). Developing learning groups that are truly contributive enhances students' abilities to interdependently consolidate deeper learning by teaching their newly acquired knowledge to their peers. So how can one get started developing successful groups?

A classic method for developing contributive learning groups is called the jigsaw strategy. In 1971, Elliot Aronson developed the jigsaw method to accelerate learning performance among students in recently desegregated schools. Since then, it has been used extensively as a means to equitably empower learners of all types. Think of the jigsaw method as a sort of deconstructive approach to contributive learning. A large amount of content is broken up into more digestible chunks by the members of a contributive learning group and then put back together to form a complete picture of the whole. This is the essence of discovering synergy between people with disparate yet complementary background knowledge and skills.

By narrowing their focus, students are able to go much deeper into a single portion of the new content they are learning. Students are then better able to use the content-specific language they have acquired to teach what they have just learned to everyone in the group, consolidating a deeper collective understanding. This process is then repeated by each member until the entire group has attained mastery of the new content. By adding their unique piece of understanding to the group, every member contributes to the process of generating meaning and deeper understanding.

TOOLS FOR CONTRIBUTIVE LEARNING

Each member of a contributive group is an expert in just one part of the whole, but when each part is combined, the sum is far greater than any one of the parts. A helpful analogy for thinking about the jigsaw learning method in a group format is to consider how the individual athletes on championship teams leverage their unique talents and skills to contribute to the whole group.

You can use a more contributive version of the KND graphic organizer in Jamboard to help scaffold this process. One type of contributive learning group involves pairs of learners. Two students can use the Learning Pairs Jigsaw Jamboard. Have two learning partners divide new learning content into two equal halves or chunks. Have students start by identifying what each needs to know in the top field.

LEARNING PAIRS JIGSAW JAMBOARD

For example, two students, Donna and Bobby, contribute what each knows in order to help each other reach the learning goal of understanding and explaining the similarities and differences between metamorphic, igneous, and sedimentary rocks.

COMPLETED LEARNING PAIRS JIGSAW JAMBOARD

We need to understand and explain the differences and similarities between metamorphic, igneous, and sedimentary rock.

Donna — My Chunk:
- Igneous
- Metamorphic
- Sedimentary
- Granite is metamorphic
- Igneous rocks start hot and then cool
- Sandstone is sedimentary
- Igneous rocks can change into metamorphic
- **Obsidian is igneous**
- Sedimentary rocks start as small particles

Bobby — My Chunk:
- Magama
- Granite is metamorphic
- Metamorphic rocks start as another type or rock, then change
- Sedimentary
- Flint is sedimentary
- Sedimentary rocks can change into metamorphic rocks
- **Shale**
- Limestone is sedimentary
- Sedimentary rocks are layered

The first partner reads or interacts with the first chunk of new content (it could be a video, multimedia file, or online source of content knowledge and information), while the second partner interacts with the second chunk of new content. Using the Learning Pairs Jigsaw Jamboard, each partner individually identifies important new terms, facts, and ideas gleaned from the content and inputs them as separate sticky notes in each half of their Jamboard. Each partner can then organize the new terms, facts, and ideas into categories based on their importance.

Once again, consider using these sentence stems to help guide students through this process:

> "_____ and _____ are alike because they both _____."

Or,

> "_____ and _____ are not alike because _____ is _____, but _____ is _____."

Once each item is categorized, the learning pair can combine their inferential reasoning capabilities. This will potentially double their capacity to identify new patterns or trends of similarities and differences between their collective prior knowledge and new learning content.

At times, you may find yourself in a learning "trio" where three people can break apart a larger amount of content into three equal subcategories. Follow the same process using the Learning Trio Jigsaw Jamboard. As before, each member of the learning trio adds important new terms, facts, and ideas to their portion of the Jamboard. Then they follow the same steps of categorizing the new sticky notes based on the similarities and differences between members' prior knowledge and this new knowledge. The key difference is that now you will potentially have access to three times the collective background knowledge. This is a broader foundation that can be leveraged to draw inferences, craft elaborations, and provide evidence to support the group's collective understanding of the new content.

Other times you'll be fortunate enough to be in a four-part learning group. This time, the group will divide an even larger amount of content into four equal chunks. Each person will add new terms, facts, and ideas to their portion of the Four-Part Jigsaw Jamboard and group these items into logical categories. However, now the contributive learning group has quadrupled the potential prior knowledge base that can be leveraged to better understand this new content and make meaningful connections and elaborations.

LEARNING TRIO JIGSAW JAMBOARD

What do we NEED to know? [Add Text]

Name: My Chunk — New Term, New Fact, New Idea (×3)

Name: My Chunk — New Term, New Fact, New Idea (×3)

Name: My Chunk — New Term, New Fact, New Idea (×3)

FOUR-PART JIGSAW JAMBOARD

What do we NEED to know? [Add Text]

Name: My Chunk — New Term, New Fact, New Idea (multiple)

Name: My Chunk — New Term, New Fact, New Idea (multiple)

Name: My Chunk — New Term, New Fact, New Idea (multiple)

Name: My Chunk — New Term, New Fact, New Idea (multiple)

MAKING A HABIT OF CONTRIBUTIVE LEARNING

Measuring Your Zone-ness

THE ZONE-NESS SCALE

MASTERY SCORE	INDICATOR
3	Mastering: I am agilely and mindfully implementing this strategy to develop my "zone-ness."
2	Developing: I am close to agilely and mindfully implementing this strategy to develop my "zone-ness."
1	Beginning: I am committed to implementing this strategy to develop my "zone-ness."

Guiding Questions
Meta-Habit #4: Engaging in Contributive Learning

Regarding the habit of contributive learning:
1. Where do you currently fall on the zone-ness scale?
2. Where do you want to be on the zone-ness scale?
3. What will you do to get there?
4. How will you know when you get there?
5. How will you express and represent this to others?

CONCLUSION

The research is abundantly clear: humans learn better together than we do in isolation. As a budding guitarist, I learned adequately on my own, but I was able to learn new chords, progressions, songs, and riffs much faster when I became a member of a contributive learning group.

This meta-learning habit, like each habit, is significantly enhanced when new learning content is logically organized into some larger contextual framework. In the next chapter, we'll explore the fifth meta-learning habit of using learning frameworks to generate greater collective understanding and efficacy.

6
MAKING A HABIT OF USING LEARNING FRAMEWORKS

If you want to be a great guitarist, you need to know that you're in one stage of development and you've got to learn how to get to the next level.

—Eddie Van Halen

Becoming a member of a contributive learning group is an important meta-habit. But how can we make sure that *everyone* in the group optimizes their learning? The answer seems to lie with framing the entire learning process itself. Frameworks are powerful cognitive scaffolds that help optimize the process of learning new content in particular and learning in general. Frameworks provide necessary context that helps us see the bigger picture of our current status, where we've been, and where we want to go. This helps us better understand our proximity to mastery and what we need to do to get there.

I was very lucky to have learned something of value, indirectly of course, from one of the most innovative rock guitarists of all time. The first learning framework I ever used was Eddie Van Halen's guitar-playing framework.

UNCLE EDDIE'S FRAMEWORK

By the spring of 1978, my guitar-playing friends and I had acquired driver's licenses. We would routinely go down to the mysterious Pine Barrens or the beaches of the Jersey Shore to play music around campfires. One afternoon, on our way to one such gathering, a friend told me he had a tape of a new band he wanted me to hear. He popped it into the eight-track player of his souped-up Chevy Nova, and the sound that emerged from those enormous speakers changed my life forever.

The eight-track was Van Halen's self-titled studio album, their first. The track was a song called "Eruption." It was like a swift kick to the head. I'd never heard anything like it. My mouth dropped open in sheer amazement of this guitar wizardry. I had no idea that those kinds of sounds could be produced by a single electric guitar. The mad genius behind all of it? The legendary Eddie Van Halen.

How was it possible to make a guitar sound like that? This was uncharted territory for me. Eddie's masterful fretwork was rendered on a guitar that he built specifically to produce a tone unlike any other guitar that had previously existed. It was mesmerizing. "Eruption" took me completely out of my comfort zone. I knew I couldn't go back to just playing the same old songs over and over again. I had to learn more.

A short time later, I heard Eddie Van Halen as the special guest on DJ John DeBella's popular show on a local Philadelphia rock radio station. Eddie was in town to perform at the Spectrum in Philadelphia. He was humble, funny, and clearly having the time of his life as a guitar god. Then DeBella asked him a question that is forever burned on my brain: "Eddie, do you have any advice for budding guitar players here in the Delaware Valley?"

Eddie paused for a moment, and when he responded, all humor was gone from his voice. I have replayed what he said in my head so many times that I can recall it as if it were yesterday. I remember Eddie saying, "Yeah, I do, John." Then, addressing the listeners, he continued, "Kids, this is your Uncle Eddie talking. If you're learning to play guitar then you're probably playing songs on the guitar that you know from the radio, or maybe you bought a book and learned to play songs with open chords and are singing along. That's how I started. That's how every great guitarist started. But..." He paused for moment. "If you want to get better, you have to know that you're in a stage. It's a stage that I call the 'campfire stage,' because you're probably sitting around a campfire strumming your guitar, playing songs that you learned from the radio, making friends and meeting new people, and that's great."

I felt as though Eddie were talking directly to me.

"Every guitarist," Eddie went on, "has gone through the campfire stage. But in order to be a *great* guitarist, you have to go through another stage—one that I call the 'Chuck Berry stage.' Every *great* guitarist has gone through the Chuck Berry stage of guitar playing. You've got to learn how to rock and roll like Chuck. You've got to learn how to play all those great rock riffs and licks like the back of your hand."

John DeBella chimed in then, saying, "Okay, so there's a campfire stage and a Chuck Berry stage. Is there another stage?"

Eddie was almost reverential when he said, "The next stage is the most important stage. It's also the hardest one to get to. That's when you invent a new way of playing that is all your own. Once you get to that stage, you are all by yourself, and it's amazing. But you've got to *really* want it. You've got to work hard to get there. You can't fake it."

Three stages of learning guitar: campfire, Chuck Berry, and Eddie Van Halen. I clearly knew that I was in the first stage. I also clearly knew that, if I wanted to get better, I would have to start learning how to rock on the guitar like Chuck Berry. That was my next stage. I immediately bought my first Chuck Berry record and set about learning how to play his greatest hits. I was taking a deeper dive into understanding the foundational patterns of rock music by learning how Chuck Berry transformed Mississippi Delta blues into an entirely new genre of music—rock and roll. Chuck Berry's signature licks inspired every would-be guitar player who followed in his footsteps. Learning how to play "Rock and Roll Music," "Roll Over Beethoven," and of course, "Johnny B. Goode" consumed me.

That interview forever altered my view of learning. In just a few minutes, Eddie Van Halen gave me a conceptual framework that, to this day, helps me think about learning to learn music. His guitar-playing framework was a lens that provided a meaningful context to my learning journey. It also offered milestones from which I could gain helpful feedback to determine how close I was to achieving my goals. I could readily see that I was in the initial stage of learning, the campfire stage. I wanted to get better, so I knew that I had to invest the time and energy to learn how to play like Chuck Berry before I could attain the highest stage, in which I was inventing a new style of music that was all my own. *I made a habit of leveraging conceptual frameworks to provide context for my learning journeys.*

THE DESIRE FOR ORDER

Using conceptual frameworks nurtures the emotional mind by helping us make sense out of confusing and therefore uncomfortable circumstances. Humans like things to be organized. We generally prefer to have some type of logical order in the world around us, because that makes us feel secure. Chaos, on the other hand, generally causes us to feel discomfort. Fortunately, the human brain's affinity for patterns is coupled with a distinct attraction to orderliness. Generally speaking, humans have an innate need for closure, and so it appears that a substantial portion of our higher-order executive brain functioning seeks the path of least resistance from some chaotic state to a more orderly one. We don't feel fully at ease until we've crossed the chasm from chaos to control (Medina 2008).

To make that leap we first need a crystal-clear picture of our current level of mastery. Frameworks with clear, unambiguous stages help us to more meaningfully understand where we are in the context of the bigger picture—our mastery learning journey. Clear and unambiguous stages also help us to be more honest with ourselves about the "here and now." It takes a certain amount of self-acceptance, even courage, to identify and address any shortcomings. Learning how to delay our gratification and invest our efforts in identifying, clarifying, and rectifying these shortcomings leads to payoffs that are real, compounding, and sustainable.

The process of mastering some new learning challenge allows us to consolidate declarative and procedural knowledge—what we know and what we can do—into our more permanent memory system. Our brains release their neurochemical cocktail of dopamine, serotonin, oxytocin, and even endorphin to generate good feelings when we finally master some new knowledge or skill that has eluded us (Breuning 2018). That mental celebration of success positively reinforces our constant quest to make sense of nonsensical situations. That is the essence of the learning journey. Attaining a level of mastery brings closure to the chaos of misunderstanding that we experience at the beginning of any mastery learning journey.

Conceptual frameworks also nurture our cognitive minds by providing guideposts along the route of our mastery journeys. Eddie Van Halen's guitar-playing framework gave me distinct stages that I could use to assess my progress on my journey toward mastery. The identification of these three distinct stages was not only innovative but self-evident, because it made perfect sense the first time I heard it. I clearly understood that I was in the campfire stage of playing, because my own characteristics in this stage perfectly matched Eddie's description. Putting my learning into a more orderly context helped me to better understand my own experiences. Knowing that I was in the first of three distinct stages also helped me to realize the limitations of my current stage of learning and that I had a lot of work to do in order to progress to the next level.

This created a new type of cognitive tension. While I was happy with my progress up to that point, the knowledge that there was a lot more to learn in order to improve created an internal conflict. I was no longer satisfied to keep playing the same songs over and over again. Having a clear picture of my current performance as well as the next level I aspired to attain was like holding two opposing thoughts in my mind simultaneously. These two contrary stages generated a kind of creative tension that I simply had to resolve in order to gain closure. This creative tension gave rise to newfound energy, which compelled me to find the path of least resistance to move forward. In order to rock out like Chuck Berry—to rise to a new level of mastery—I had to plan, think, and act more intentionally about my playing.

Eddie's framework also helped me to understand the critical importance of attaining a "mastery orientation." If something was worth doing, then it was worth doing to the best of my abilities. For the first time, I recognized that I wanted to align my efforts toward mastery and not just playing campfire songs that required less and less effort. The shift for me was that I wanted to gain a deeper understanding of Chuck Berry's effortless artistry, and so I would have to work even harder but also work *much differently*. It was a long road ahead, and I was reaching for much more difficult skills. I needed better learning strategies. That simple recognition illuminated a pathway forward. It compelled me to implement, modify, and evaluate the impact that new learning strategies had on building my new skill set.

Eddie Van Halen's guitar-playing framework worked more like a compass than a map. It didn't spell out exactly what I needed to do. Rather, the identification of the three stages of mastery helped me establish a heading so I could continue in the right direction. It also provided clear and distinct stages of learning that allowed me to detail my progress as I designed *my own route* to my desired destination.

WHAT MAKES A LEARNING FRAMEWORK USEFUL?

The British mathematician George E. P. Box once said that all models are false, but some models are useful. The challenge is being able to discern models that are false but useful from those that are false and useless. This is the goal of social science research in places where human beings interact—like schools. The process by which humans learn and make meaning is a phenomenon that is remarkably complex, and it is influenced by an astonishing array of uncontrollable variables. It is impossible to perfectly represent every facet of human learning with conceptual models or frameworks. This fundamental problem explains what Box meant when he said that all models are false.

One way that educational researchers tackle this problem is by implementing strict scientific methods and tools to intentionally reduce as many errors and biases as possible. This rigorous process helps researchers better understand and clarify the conditional relationships between learners, the learning content, and the context in which that learning takes place. Learning frameworks that are built from ample educational research are still false—because there are just too many variables—but they are far more likely to be *useful*. Useful models help illuminate larger patterns of relationships that we would otherwise miss. They give us perspective. This helps us to better understand critical aspects of human learning conditions and how to most reliably optimize them. What follows is an overview of two highly useful frameworks and a new model to help us find our optimal learning zone.

THE VISIBLE LEARNING MODEL

John Hattie (2008) is an educational researcher whose Visible Learning model is built upon decades of rigorous educational research, making it one of the most well-known, and useful, models for framing the human learning process. The Visible Learning model identifies three distinct stages of learning: surface learning, deeper learning, and knowledge transfer. According to Hattie's model, all learning begins with surface-level interaction with new knowledge. At this level, we begin to acquire the basic rudiments of learning by committing content-specific vocabulary terms, basic details, and simple facts to memory. It is an essential step, but it's only the first step.

THE VISIBLE LEARNING MODEL

At the deeper learning stage, the surface details we memorized need to be leveraged to better understand more complex concepts and ideas about the new content. At this stage of learning, we also need to compare our prior knowledge to the new knowledge we seek to more deeply understand. By acquiring a deeper level of understanding, we actually consolidate the surface-level knowledge we have previously acquired into our long-term memory system. But in order to consolidate deeper knowledge, we have to progress to the third level of learning, in which we apply our deeper knowledge by transferring it in some new context. It is at the knowledge-transfer stage that deeper learning is finally consolidated into our long-term retention systems. When it comes to retaining deeper learning, we have to use it, or we lose it.

Take, for example the learning goal from chapter 5, "I will understand and be able to explain the similarities and differences between metamorphic, igneous, and sedimentary rocks." At the surface level, students need to acquire the terms "metamorphic," "igneous," and "sedimentary" as well as the basic facts and details about each type of rock. At the deeper learning level, students will need to be able to explain and elaborate on the similarities and differences both within and between these categories without any critical errors or omissions. At the knowledge-transfer level, students will need to be able to apply their new understanding by generating new insights and inferences that can be used to solve challenges or problems in different contexts.

THE T3 FRAMEWORK

John Hattie's Visible Learning model provides highly reliable guidance on how to positively influence learning performance. However, the digital age offers an entirely new frontier of possibilities for accelerating learning with digital learning tools. Such an exciting prospect warrants an approach that exploits the potential of digital tools to optimize learning performance in whole systems.

THE T3 FRAMEWORK

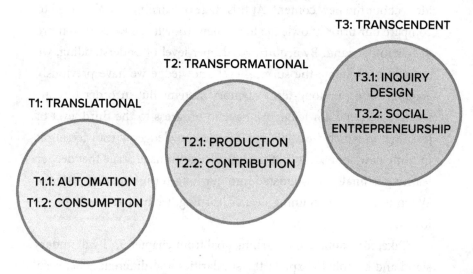

My primary objective for writing the book *Disruptive Classroom Technologies: A Framework for Innovation in Education* was to offer a common and actionable language for innovative teaching and learning practices with digital technologies. In it, I introduced the T3 Framework for Innovation in Education. The T3 Framework provides a highly reliable pathway for modern learning systems that was driven by years of rigorous research (Magana 2017). The T3 Framework increments the impact of using digital tools into three hierarchical domains: translational, transformational, and transcendent.

Translational learning reflects the most common ways that digital tools are used in learning environments. Translating tasks from an analog to a digital form adds some value in terms of increasing efficiency, accuracy, and time savings, but it has little impact on improving learning performance. Translational learning tasks include automating presentations, test taking, and consuming digital content from online sources or other electronic media. This is a necessary first stage, but all too often school systems make the mistake of stopping there.

Transformational learning converts learners from passive consumers of content to active knowledge creators and contributors. Transformational learning strategies help learners use digital technologies to embrace a mastery orientation by first developing mastery learning goals and then mindfully monitoring and regulating the impact of their emotions, effort, and progress toward those goals using the Magana Mastery Tracker. At this deeper level of learning, students use digital tools for becoming more engaged in planning for their learning, creatively expressing and representing what they know and can do, and making their thinking visible to themselves and others.

Transcendent learning pushes past the boundaries of expectations for educational systems. Transcendent learning strategies include students identifying, investigating, and hypothesizing more robust solutions to wicked problems that matter to them. Instead of solving problems that are given to them, at the transcendent level of learning, students learn to identify and investigate complex real-world problems. They apply or transfer their newly gained knowledge as leverage to make improvements in their world. In the process, students gain valuable social-entrepreneurship skills that help them become far more future ready. This entirely new educational model is only possible when learners mindfully wield digital technologies to make their world a better place, solving one wicked problem at a time.

We are only just beginning to scratch the surface of what's possible when students' limitless passion and purpose for improving their world are catalyzed in educational settings. T3 Framework research has been peer reviewed by a host of global education scholars and was recently published in the *Oxford Research Encyclopedia of Education*, making T3 a highly reliable and useful model for improving modern learning (Magana 2019).

Conducting rigorous educational research is complex work—but so is interpreting and implementing research-based findings and strategies with fidelity. So, can all of these complicated findings and strategies be distilled into a memorable framework that any learner can use to find their optimum learning zone?

THE LEARNING MAZE

I'd like to introduce a new and more student-centric learning model derived from ancient Greek mythology: the learning maze.

In Greek mythology, the tyrannical King Minos ruled the island of Crete with an iron fist. King Minos was tasked by the gods with caring for the mighty Minotaur, a mythical beast with a bull's head and man's body. The tormented Minotaur was imprisoned in an elaborate maze-like structure, the labyrinth, beneath King Minos's palace. The labyrinth was designed and built by the architect Daedalus and his ill-fated son, Icarus, and was said to be so confusing that Daedalus and Icarus barely escaped their own maze. As the story goes, the Minotaur would eat human sacrifices every three years. So, every three years, seven fair maidens and seven young men were gathered from across Greece to be sacrificed to the Minotaur. Once they entered the labyrinth, none were heard from again.

One year, King Aegeus of Athens was ordered to send his heroic young son, Theseus, along with thirteen other Athenians to be sacrificed to the Minotaur. Distraught, Aegeus was compelled to comply with the order to sacrifice his son or suffer the wrath of the gods. So, Theseus sailed off to the island of Crete to meet his fate along with his fellow Athenians at the center of the labyrinth. But, as luck would have it, once he landed on Crete, Theseus caught the eye of King Minos's daughter, the beautiful Ariadne. The flame-haired Ariadne fell in love with the handsome young prince at first sight. Ariadne couldn't bear to think of losing her new love to the Minotaur, so she hatched an ingenious plot to save him.

On the night before he was to be sacrificed, Ariadne snuck into Theseus's chambers bearing two gifts: a sword and a ball of red string comprised entirely of her own hair. Grateful for the sword, but puzzled by the hair ball, Theseus implored Ariadne to help him make sense of these implements. The sword, said Ariadne, was a mighty weapon that Theseus could use to slay the unsuspecting Minotaur. She then explained that Theseus should attach one end of the hair twine to the opening of the labyrinth and unravel it, bit by bit, so that he and his fellow Athenians could keep track of their route to the center of the labyrinth. As long as the thread remained unbroken, Theseus was sure to find his way out of the labyrinth. This plan worked perfectly for Theseus, who slayed the Minotaur then led his compatriots safely out of the labyrinth, retracing their steps to daylight by following Ariadne's thread.

The learning maze is a simplified, but apt model to describe the surface, deep, and knowledge-transfer stages of learning. When we encounter a new learning problem, much like a new learning maze, we have to first observe and orient ourselves at the opening or surface of the maze. We need to use memorization strategies to acquire the basic tools, like new terms, basic facts, and ideas, to help us become oriented to the maze. We have to acquire these surface learning tools so that we can apply them and proceed deeper into the learning maze.

To reach the deeper levels of the learning maze, like Theseus, we have to use a different set of tools than we used at the surface of the maze. Memorization techniques are no match for deeper learning. Instead, we must use the tools of logic, inferential reasoning, and prior knowledge to more deeply understand the larger concept, "slaying" our former ignorance about these complex ideas in the process.

But we can't stop there. We have to exit the learning maze, and so we need to use a different set of learning tools than we used in either the surface level or the deeper level. We have to learn how to transfer our deeper learning, using it as a new tool to solve other problems—like helping others learn what we have just mastered. Only then can we follow Ariadne's metaphorical thread of logic, exiting the learning maze as a learner transformed, a learner with a higher level of cognizance and consciousness.

T3 LEARNING MAZE PLANNING GUIDE

Consider using the T3 Learning Maze Planning Guide to help scaffold how you put the learning-maze metaphor into practice in your classrooms. This planning tool will help guide how you differentiate your instructional design and planning into the three phases of learning: surface, deep, and knowledge transfer or "transcendent" learning. Breaking down your planning to correspond with these three phases of learning will help you identify teaching strategies, activities, and tools that are specifically designed for each phase.

T3. APPLIED LEARNING PLAN:
What will I do to help students demonstrate, model, and communicate surface learning and deeper understanding free from critical errors or oversights?

T1. SURFACE LEARNING PLAN:
What will I do to help students acquire key vocabulary, facts, and details free from critical errors or oversights?

T3 LEARNING MAZE PLANNING GUIDE

T2. DEEPER LEARNING PLAN:
What will I do to help students categorize surface learning details to identify similarities and differences and new patterns that emerge so they can make elaborations and provide evidence to support their claims?

The questions in each text field of the guide will help you think about what teaching strategies and activities you can sequence to improve learning at all three phases. This will not only save you time but will help align the strategies and learning experiences you select that assist students in acquiring foundational or surface knowledge, deepening their learning, and applying their new knowledge in different contexts. This will also give your students the opportunity to think creatively and critically, communicate, and contribute to others' learning by choosing how to represent their own understanding. These student-generated assessments could be tutorials that students create to teach others what they know, learning flash cards that they create in Quizlet, games they develop in Scratch, or learning worlds they create in Minecraft. The sky's the limit. Just giving students the opportunity to represent their knowledge gain in their own ways will amplify their voice, choice, and confidence.

MAKING A HABIT OF USING LEARNING FRAMEWORKS 97

T3. APPLIED LEARNING PLAN:
1. Individual learning storyboard
2. Post-assessment with quizzes
3. Student-generated assessments

T1. SURFACE LEARNING PLAN:
1. KND chart with small groups
2. Pre-assessment memorization games with quizzes
3. Frayer graphic organizer

T3 LEARNING MAZE PLANNING GUIDE

T2. DEEPER LEARNING PLAN:
1. Learning Group Deeper Learning Slide Deck
2. Venn Diagram Graphic Organizer for similarities and differences
3. Learning storyboard with evidence for claims

Measuring Your Zone-ness

THE ZONE-NESS SCALE

MASTERY SCORE	INDICATOR
3	Mastering: I am agilely and mindfully implementing this strategy to develop my "zone-ness."
2	Developing: I am close to agilely and mindfully implementing this strategy to develop my "zone-ness."
1	Beginning: I am committed to implementing this strategy to develop my "zone-ness".

Guiding Questions
Meta-Habit #5: Using Learning Frameworks

Regarding the habit of using learning frameworks:

1. Where do you currently fall on the zone-ness scale?
2. Where do you want to be on the zone-ness scale?
3. What will you do to get there?
4. How will you know when you get there?
5. How will you express and represent this to others?

CONCLUSION

As a student, I spent a lot of time in school just superficially covering content with a minimum-proficiency orientation. A minimum-proficiency orientation is perfectly suited for the cram-and-jam game of memorization and regurgitation, but it was useless for helping me get closer to my optimum learning zone. When it came to learning music, the epiphany of Eddie Van Halen's guitar-playing framework inspired me to develop the meta-learning habit of contextualizing my learning by using frameworks to guide my learning journeys.

Some learning mazes may be similar to others, but no two are identical. Each journey to the center of some new learning maze produces both new knowledge and a greater awareness of how to optimize knowledge generation by providing an opportunity for reflecting upon our collection of previously mastered learning mazes. In the next chapter, we'll explore the why, what, and how of the next meta-learning habit: making imaginative connections, categorizing our learning, and deeply reflecting on our actions.

7

MAKING A HABIT OF CONNECTING, CATEGORIZING, AND REFLECTING

> *Making mental connections is our most crucial learning tool, the essence of human intelligence; to forge links; to go beyond the given; to see patterns, relationships, context.*
>
> —Marilyn Ferguson

Eddie Van Halen's guitar-playing framework, like the learning-maze metaphor, proved enormously helpful for finding my optimum learning zone. I now had the tools to more confidently explore and learn the vast range of musical genres, taking me far beyond three-chord rock songs. I began to develop the meta-learning habit of mentally organizing my musical learning mazes into categories and then larger clusters, making and extending connections within and between each and then deeply reflecting on my entire learning process.

EXPANDING MY REPERTOIRE

My capacity to play guitar grew enormously when I built on my foundational knowledge, but using Eddie Van Halen's guitar-playing framework gave me a meaningful meta-organizational framework for contextualizing my musical growth and progress. I knew I would always be working toward that elusive, transcendent stage at which I formed my own style of musical expression. But I became more acutely aware of a pattern or sequence of strategies that helped me optimize how to learn new songs by making connections between songs I was learning with songs I already knew, categorizing groups of songs based on their similarities, and deeply reflecting upon and adding to my repertoire of learning strategies.

During this period, I was playing and performing with new musicians regularly. They exposed me to a vast world of musical forms that they loved. This naturally led me to explore musical styles that I simply would not have otherwise considered. With so many musical genres in which to get lost, I needed to organize my growing body of knowledge into some sort of schema.

I discovered that applying my ability to learn new songs more efficiently made it significantly easier to expand and diversify my repertoire. That organization helped me maintain conceptual classifications of music that I was exploring. For example, the pentatonic—or five-tone—scales, featured in nearly every rock solo, were really adaptations and improvisations of the blues scales I memorized from Chuck Berry's riffs. I made the connection that all those blues scales were grounded in the music of the blues. I started to pursue a deeper understanding of the origins and meaning of the blues. I began to more fully appreciate the human story—the devastating toll of bondage and oppression that was voiced through the characteristic call-and-answer phrasing—of the blues. The more I learned about the blues, the more I learned how the *feelings* that were evoked by the musical stories in the blues connected powerfully to something inherently human—sadness, loneliness, longing. It seemed like I was learning an entirely new grammar of musical expression.

I began identifying the patterns that made a song fit into superordinate (larger) clusters or subordinate (smaller) categories. For example a song that belonged to the superordinate cluster of the Blues might also fit into a unique subordinate category such as Delta blues, Chicago Blues, electric blues, or acoustic blues. Grouping blues songs into these subordinate categories based on their stylistic similarities and differences gave me a much better understanding of what type of song I was learning to play and how to best play it. The blues became a superordinate cluster into which I could mentally organize subordinate styles of songs any way I wanted. The process of classifying songs into superordinate clusters and subordinate categories proved tremendously helpful for keeping track of all the songs I was learning and playing.

Mentally organizing music also allowed me to learn how to transpose a song from one musical cluster into the style of an entirely different cluster. For example, Bob Dylan's classic folk-rock song "Knocking on Heaven's Door" was performed by Eric Clapton in a reggae style that stands as one of the greatest covers of all time. I learned how to reimagine and perform my favorite songs in different styles. I discovered that learning how to become an agile musician was all about recognizing the sonic patterns of songs, classifying them into some relevant organizational system that made sense to me, and then being able to alternate between those different systems. My repertoire expanded enormously.

I was keenly aware that I was developing a higher level of musical awareness. Creating an organizational schema of superordinate clusters and subordinate categories helped me make lasting mental connections of the musical learning mazes I had experienced, and brought me even closer to my optimum learning zone. Making mental connections seemed like a natural way to organize my thinking and my learning. Ultimately, this habit helped me to organize any new knowledge that I wanted to learn. *I made a habit of organizing new knowledge clusters by making mental connections, categorizing those connections, and reflecting on the entire process.*

FINDING THE PATH

Organizing my musical learning journeys into interconnected clusters and categories nourished my emotional mind. I was initially daunted by the incredible variety of music that I was learning and discovering. There was so much to know and learn that it was sometimes tempting to procrastinate or even give up trying to make sense of it all. But the path from chaos to control was brought into sharper focus by believing in my own capacity to learn how to optimize my learning, regardless of the content.

Keeping track of my ever-expanding music repertoire was quite challenging at first. Imagining a higher-level organizing scheme made me feel more assured about myself and my learning capacity. If I could find pathways through new musical learning mazes, I could apply the same meta-habits to any learning maze, regardless of the content, which I did with great results. Successfully transferring this meta-learning habit into other subject areas was empowering for me as a learner. It also helped me to gain confidence in my ability to take on greater learning challenges and explore new ways of expressing and representing my knowledge gain.

Making and extending my musical connections also helped me to vary how I practiced new songs. I started aligning my style of playing to the cluster of music I was learning. For example, I took a completely different approach or strategy for learning how to play a classic rock song than I did with a Latin-infused rock song, a Southern rock song, or a country waltz. I developed and learned how to finesse a new range of musical phrases and styles, like flat picking, finger picking, or bending and sustaining high notes, depending on the musical genre I was learning to play. Over time and with ample practice, I kept adding new phrases into my musical vocabulary. Consequently, I was also adding new tools and strategies into my pattern-literacy toolbox. Learning how to use just the right learning tool at just the right time is a key element of finding one's optimum learning zone.

Reflecting on the totality of my learning was also exceedingly satisfying. I would make the time to deeply reflect on the new scales, tones, and patterns I was learning. I would visualize the scale patterns on the guitar fretboard in my mind's eye. If I was struggling with a certain riff or solo, I would imagine myself playing it correctly and in time. I wouldn't necessarily dwell on my mistakes, but I did reflect upon them in order to reduce the errors I made. Then I would break down this whole process into segments, practice each segment until I mastered it, and then proceed to the next segment. The process of reflecting on my learning and playing helped to reinforce the impact of strategies I was applying and whether or not they were effective. My musical learning journal became filled with ideas, notes, doodles, and all sorts of little cognitive organizers that helped me accelerate my learning in ways that were otherwise impossible.

Developing a habit of organizing categories of music into clusters also nurtured my cognitive mind. As I made more mental connections between superordinate clusters and subordinate categories of genres and songs, I was actually developing and strengthening neural networks in my brain. As mentioned in chapter 4, immersive experiential learning thickens the myelin sheathing surrounding the neurons in our brains and increases the speed at which bio-chemical-electrical signals travel up and down neurons and neuronal networks. Therefore, with each new mental connection I made, extended, and reflected upon, I was encoding learning experiences into my permanent neurological networks.

WHAT DOES CONNECTING, CATEGORIZING, AND REFLECTING LOOK LIKE?

When I learn a new song, I start with the notes. I like to consider each note like a new term that is unique unto itself. Then I arrange those notes to form larger riffs or melodic motifs. Then I organize those riffs into larger melodic phrases. Then I organize those phrases into categories of songs by my favorite artists, like the Allman Brothers, Eric Clapton, Mark Knopfler, or the Beatles. Then I organize those songs into larger clusters of music, like classic rock, Southern rock, blues, or soul. Notes, motifs, phrases, songs, song categories, and genres. That's the organizational structure that I've come to use to help me keep track of all the wonderful music I've grown to love and play.

It may not come as a surprise that in high school I became very interested in learning about biological sciences and, particularly, the structure of taxonomies of life forms. I learned that in the eighteenth century a Swedish botanist named Carl Linnaeus developed an elegant system for clustering organisms based on their similarities and differences that has become a pillar of the biological sciences. The Linnaean system is really a clustering taxonomy with seven superordinate headings: kingdom, phylum, class, order, family, genus, and species. Within each of these superordinate groups were subordinate categories of organisms with similar characteristics. This taxonomy is used to organize all life forms, which is really remarkable. For example, we all belong to the genus *Homo* and the species *sapiens*; but we also belong to the family of Hominids, or organisms with humanlike facial characteristics and vision. We have grasping fingers and collar bones, so we belong to the Primate order. We also have hair, backbones, and the ability to move on our own, and so we belong to the class Mammalia, the phylum Chordata, and the kingdom Animalia.

I applied my music-organization scheme to a parallel taxonomy of learning as a *clustering scheme* that I use to help me better connect, extend, and reflect upon my learning in science and other subjects.

I start with the fundamentals, like key terms. Then I organize those terms into larger facts about the learning content. Then I organize those facts into larger ideas or concepts. Then I organize those ideas into larger categories. Finally, I organize those categories into even larger clusters. In the next section, we'll play around with this mental structure to create organizational schemata that make sense to you.

T3 LEARNING MAZE GOAL PLANNER

Implementing graphic organizers is a powerful way to help scaffold the process of categorizing, connecting, and reflecting upon learning for students (Marzano and Pickering 2001). Graphic organizers, such as Venn diagrams, assist learners in how they interact with and organize new knowledge they have acquired. Consider using—or modifying—the Learning Maze Goal Planner to help students deconstruct mastery learning goals into the three phases of learning: surface learning goals, deeper learning goals, and applied learning goals. The process of completing the planner will help guide students in the important metacognitive process of considering, thinking about, and discussing actionable strategies that help them learn at each learning phase. Later, it will help them analyze why those strategies worked or didn't.

The Learning Maze Goal Planner graphic organizer will also help students contextualize and even capture their learning journeys so they can be connected and extended. Since the learning maze was built in Google Slides, students can add links to their completed learning products. These products can include, but should not be limited to, HyperDocs, slide shows, spreadsheets, audio files, video files, Minecraft worlds, and a whole assortment of student-generated tutorials. Students can store their graphic organizers in their Google Drive to create portfolios of actual learning products for easy access and cumulative reflection on each learning journey.

When introducing this graphic organizer to students, consider posing, and even posting, these guiding questions to help them build and align their learning strategies to specific phases of learning:

1. What learning intention do I want to master?
2. What does surface-level mastery look like? What strategies will I use at this level?
3. What does deeper-level mastery look like? What strategies will I use at this level?
4. How will I apply my knowledge? What strategies will I use at this level?

T3. APPLIED LEARNING GOAL:
What will I do to demonstrate, model, and communicate surface-level and deeper understanding free from critical errors or oversights?

T1. SURFACE LEARNING GOAL:
What will I do to learn new vocabulary terms, facts, and details without critical errors or oversights?

T3 LEARNING MAZE GOAL PLANNER

T2. DEEPER LEARNING GOAL:
What will I do to put surface learning details into categories to identify similarities and differences and new patterns that emerge? What will I do to elaborate and provide evidence to support my claims?

CLUSTER-GORIES

Our knowledge vault, or the core of our actualized knowledge—the accumulated knowledge that we have acquired and consolidated over time—is the basis for all the knowledge connections we make in our lifetimes. This core is a mash-up of the concrete experiences, our abstract thoughts, and learning maze journeys that we have actualized. The more we deeply reflect upon what we know and how we came to know it, the more effectively we will fortify the neural networks that comprise this knowledge base.

The Cluster-Gories Jamboard can help students scaffold their reflective learning practices. Start with asking students to reflect upon some challenging learning maze that they have recently mastered. Then, have the students use sticky notes in the Cluster-Gories Jamboard to capture the surface-level details they consolidated—the terms, simple details, and basic facts that are now a part of their permanent selves. Students should then record the deeper conceptual understanding they gained, the new connections they established, the insights they drew, and the inferences that they made. Finally, have students record how they transferred or applied the knowledge gained from this learning maze to do or achieve something that they could not have without experiencing this particular learning maze.

This Jamboard is really an interactive metacognitive graphic organizer to help students keep track of all the learning maze artifacts they gather on their meta-learning journeys. A good example of this is the first slide with the heading "What did I NEED to know?" Use it to ask students to think about a recent learning maze they successfully completed. Have your students work in pairs or small groups to create sticky notes to capture the foundational terms, simple facts, and basic ideas that they learned.

CLUSTER-GORIES

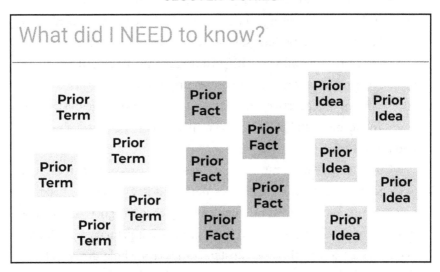

The next task is to have students organize their completed learning mazes into categories that make sense to them. For example, students might have completed learning journeys that focused on mastering addition, subtraction, multiplication, and division. Each learning journey is clearly distinct, but since they all focus on developing conventions of mathematics, they could be grouped in a category labeled number sense that belongs to the superordinate cluster called Math. Other learning mazes might focus on developing an understanding of setting, character development, or story theory. These would naturally fit into a literature category that is within the larger cluster called English Language Arts. Other learning mazes that develop students' understanding of atoms and molecules, rocks and minerals, or living organisms could be organized into different subordinate categories in the larger cluster called Science. The actual categories students choose to identify matters less than the categorization process itself. Just be sure that your students are intentional about their reasoning for the groupings and have a clear rationale for creating the category that makes sense to them.

Have your students navigate to slide 2 in the Cluster-Gories Jamboard to start creating categories for their learning mazes along with the corresponding terms, facts, and ideas that they learned. This is a meta-learning scaffold to help your students develop the strategy of connecting, categorizing, and reflecting until it becomes a habit. As a result of this practice, your students will more consciously envision how to best establish their own mental connections, categories, and reflections.

Consider having your students use screen-recording tools like Screencastify to record themselves narrating key thoughts, insights, and any inferences they draw when creating each category. This can be done individually, in pairs, or in small groups. For primary-aged learners, I suggest completing the Cluster-Gories as a whole-group activity that is facilitated by the teacher. The important thing is to make both student thinking and learning visible, archivable, and accessible.

LEARNING CATEGORIES

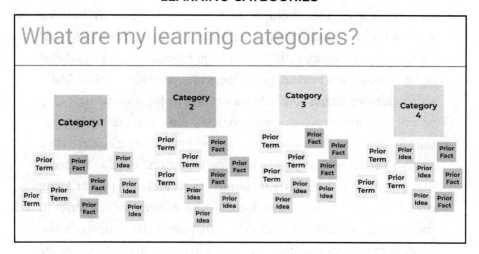

The final step is to have students mentally organize their learning categories into larger clusters. This takes students' capacity to connect, extend, and reflect upon their learning to an entirely new level. Once again, the rationale or conditions they choose for clustering their categories is entirely up to them. This will help them to better organize, connect, and extend their prior learning mazes—and add new learning tools they used to complete each learning maze to their growing learning toolbox. Over time and ample practice, this process will help your students get closer to realizing their optimal learning zone.

Have students use slide 3 in the Cluster-Gories Jamboard to help them organize the learning categories they have established into even larger clusters. Using this meta-learning scaffold will help your students maintain the discipline of implementing this strategy until it becomes a habit. Once again, they will more consciously envision establishing their own mental connections and categories with this guided reflection practice using any clustering criteria that makes sense to them.

CLUSTERS OF LEARNING CATEGORIES

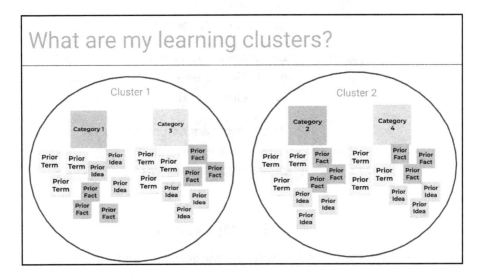

A key thing to remember here is that there is really no right or wrong way to do this. The process should be entirely up to you and your students. The Cluster-Gories Jamboard is just one way to help organize how your students build connections, categorizations, and reflections upon their learning journeys. With time and guided practice, your students will convert this organizational strategy into a meta-learning habit. That will help them to become more reflective about their prior knowledge base so that this knowledge can be more easily retrieved and leveraged to successfully explore increasingly challenging learning mazes.

Measuring Your Zone-ness

THE ZONE-NESS SCALE

MASTERY SCORE	INDICATOR
3	Mastering: I am agilely and mindfully implementing this strategy to develop my "zone-ness."
2	Developing: I am close to agilely and mindfully implementing this strategy to develop my "zone-ness."
1	Beginning: I am committed to implementing this strategy to develop my "zone-ness."

Guiding Questions

Meta-Habit #6: Connecting, Categorizing, and Reflecting

Regarding the habit of connecting, categorizing, and reflecting:

1. Where do you currently fall on the zone-ness scale?
2. Where do you want to be on the zone-ness scale?
3. What will you do to get there?

4. How will you know when you get there?
5. How will you express and represent this to others?

CONCLUSION

Developing the meta-habit of connecting, categorizing, and reflecting upon our learning maze experiences is one of the most powerful ways for us to optimize how we learn, unlearn, and relearn. Having your students construct digital knowledge museums using HyperDocs or open-ended production tools will help them build this sixth meta-learning habit with greater intentionality. While this habit increases learners' ability to encode "knowledge chunks" into their permanent selves, it also continually refines their mental organization strategies by reflecting on the selection criteria used to organize the chunks into subordinate categories and superordinate clusters.

As there are no limits to human imagination, there are also no limits as to how one can mentally organize one's learning mazes. We might imagine a book with different chapters, a computer interface with nested files, or a chest with different doors—but with room for growth. Leaners clearly benefit from a logical mental schema or rationale for organizing their learning experiences in order to retrieve just the right experience at just the right time to successfully navigate new learning mazes. The great thing is that it seems that as human beings become more successful at navigating different learning mazes, we increase the efficiency and effectiveness of our entire learning process, regardless of the type of learning maze we choose to enter.

In the next chapter, we'll take a deep dive into the final meta-learning habit: generating meta-feedback loops to more mindfully reflect *in* action and experience the awesome power of *presence*.

8
MAKING A HABIT OF META-FEEDBACK

Learners need endless feedback more than they need endless teaching.

—Grant Wiggins

Organizing my learning maze journeys into categories and then into larger clusters was enormously helpful in accelerating my learning. That mental classification system also enhanced my ability to contextualize the ways in which I reflected upon my past learning journeys. This made it easier to review the accumulation of my prior learning experiences in an ongoing way. It strengthened my neural networks and boosted my confidence in my ability to take on greater learning challenges and get closer to realizing my optimum learning zone.

When I was playing guitar with lots of other musicians, I began to experiencem the joys and challenges of live improvisation, I discovered the newfound thrill of playing in the pocket—that awesome feeling when the entire group plays in seemingly effortless synchronicity. I listened deeply to the other players' instruments in order to improvise with them. I was fully present, making music in the moment. I was used to reflection on my actions when a musical performance was over, but now I began experiencing *reflection in action*. That's when I began to develop the final meta-learning habit of generating meta-feedback.

ON FEEDBACK

At this point in my guitar learning, I was getting lots of feedback from my parents and friends about my playing. That was encouraging, but the source of the signal was someone else, not me. I became increasingly dissatisfied with the quality of that external feedback. It wasn't particularly precise, which made it less useful. I would hear comments like, "I really liked that song," or, "Dude, you sound just like Jim Croce!" While those comments gave my ego a boost, they didn't really help me improve. It's not as though my mom ever said, "You should have held that diminished chord a few beats longer before going into the bridge." The type of feedback I received from other people certainly built my confidence, but it didn't impact my learning capacity.

The timing of the feedback also seemed to matter. I wouldn't receive feedback from others until after I stopped playing, which didn't have any impact on the performance itself. I kept receiving the wrong feedback at the wrong time from the wrong source.

I realized that a more valuable type of feedback came directly from me, in the form of the sounds and tones that I was producing in the moment as a part of the whole group. Rather than only reflecting on my actions after the performance ended, I learned how to pay very close attention to what I was doing, while being mindful of the bigger picture, musically speaking. I learned to focus on how my playing sounded within the larger context of everyone else in the band. There was no feedback gap. I knew exactly how the end result should sound, so I could modify my performance in the moment to play in sync with the band. I gradually became aware of my growing ability for reflection in action regarding my own performance and the band's performance simultaneously.

This was the first time I experienced a kind of meta-feedback on the part and the whole; I was the part, and the band was the whole. I was keenly aware of both my own performance and the performance of the band—the tree and the forest—at the same time. I could modify and adjust on the fly. The real thrill was not just in playing known riffs, but in being able to improvise in the moment and anticipate what the other musicians were going to do. I found that this type of meta-feedback was a far more powerful way to play in the pocket. I was building my meta-learning capacity by becoming the source of my own meta-feedback signals. *I made a habit of generating my own meta-feedback loops to evaluate my performance in the moment.*

BEING HERE NOW

The habit of generating meta-feedback is a discipline that helps us become more fully present in all aspects our learning lives. Maintaining one's sense of presence nourishes the emotional mind. Reflecting on our action occurs *after* the moment has passed, and so its utility for improving performance during the actual moment is obviously limited. However, reflecting *in* action allows us to recognize the interplay between both the part and the whole, at once, in the midst of that performance.

Presence is the art and science of being here now. Being fully present in the moment while performing or learning enables us to transcend current circumstances, giving us a rare view of the tree and the forest at the same time. This meta-learning habit allows us to rise above our own idiosyncrasies to embrace a more inclusive and contributive frame of mind. Maintaining a presence disposition serves to shift one's perspective from the myopic to the holistic—from the isolated *me* to the connected *we*. It is from this heightened perspective that we attain transcendence.

Harnessing the power of presence makes us feel more assured in the face of—and less susceptible to—the chaos and uncertainty that surrounds every aspect of our daily lives. Gaining and maintaining a presence disposition frees up enormous amounts of psychic and cognitive energy by allowing us to transcend regrets we have about past decisions or events. Sustaining a presence disposition also serves to liberate us from any potential worries or anxieties we may harbor about what the future may hold. The combined effect frees us from distractions so that we may fully focus on optimizing our capacity for limitless learning in the here and now.

It appears that humans are naturally hardwired for maintaining a presence disposition. The art of breath control (explored in chapter 3) is a time-honored tool for achieving transcendence by maintaining the discipline of presence. Engaging in this exercise triggers our brains to positively reinforce the experience of presence by releasing an ecstasy-inducing combination of dopamine, serotonin, oxytocin, and endorphin (Breuning 2018).

In fact, the term "ecstasy" is derived from the ancient Greek word *ekstasis*, which literally means "to stand outside oneself." We gain perspective when we are able to transcend our current circumstances by standing outside ourselves and becoming conscious of the bigger picture. The meta-habit of generating meta-feedback is a pathway for achieving this goal. This higher-level perspective allows us to rise above any learning problem, gaining a higher level of consciousness than the consciousness that created the problem in the first place. This is not a trivial observation.

Generating meta-feedback by reflecting in action also nurtures our cognitive mind by strengthening our sense of efficacy—the deeply held belief that we can achieve absolutely anything. Building our self-efficacy hinges upon our ability to unlearn the habit of relying on external feedback sources and relearning how to generate our own meta-feedback signals. This is the path toward presence. It is only through presence that we synthesize all of the meta-learning habits into one complete whole and realize our limitless potential. A strong argument can be made that "present-ness" is an essential tool for attaining our optimal learning zone.

By contrast, in school, I learned the habit of relying on my classroom teachers to be the source of feedback on my learning performance. The feedback signals my teachers provided to me were typically a percentage score or letter grade on a summative examination, days or weeks after the assessment was administered. This delay dramatically reduced the reflective or metacognitive value of that feedback, and so it did little to improve my learning performance. This habit built a kind of dependence on my teachers to do all of the reflective work for me.

Learning how to play music in the moment helped me to unlearn the habit of relying on external sources of feedback and learn how to generate meta-feedback loops of my own design. This process was both joyful and empowering. The meta-feedback loops that I generated were exceedingly helpful, because I was the source of the signal, not someone or something else. This allowed me to concentrate on my part of the performance and its relationship to the whole performance simultaneously. There was no delay in the feedback return loop. This gave me a far greater sense of control and purpose as I was reflecting on the learning in the moment and how that learning related to the bigger picture of what I was trying to achieve. I was becoming cognizant of a larger, more effective meta-awareness system that I could tap into anytime I wanted.

WHAT IS META-FEEDBACK?

Meta-feedback is a higher-level information-processing system that all humans possess. Meta-feedback becomes readily available simply when one becomes aware of its existence. The trouble is that this innate capacity often goes unused, ultimately preventing us from fully learning in our optimal learning zones. The meta-feedback loop works much the same as the other feedback loops described in chapter 3: there is a source, a signal, and a recurring loop in which the signal returns to the original signal source. The key difference is that meta-feedback loops stimulate the highest level of human cognizance and perception: the meta-awareness system.

The meta-awareness system is capable of perceiving both tasks we're doing in the moment (the tree) and the larger context in which those tasks are taking place (the forest). Engaging the meta-awareness system enables us to transcend the moment and perceive the part and the whole simultaneously. It is the meta-awareness system that gives humans the extraordinary capacity to realize the awesome power of mindfulness.

There are encouraging signs indicating that education systems are beginning to make the shift from places of maximum memorization toward holistic learning systems that are focused on whole-learner well-being and mastery. This is cause for optimism in our school systems. One of the indicators of this transformation is that more focus is being placed on learning processes over learning content. We seem to be at the cusp of an educational revolution that may—hopefully—emphasize meta-learning over simple regurgitation of knowledge.

Perhaps the most encouraging indicator of this transformation is an increase in efforts toward developing mindfulness practices in K–12 education systems. There is a growing body of evidence suggesting that limitless learning capacity is a function of mindfully engaging the prefrontal cortex, the seat of executive functioning in humans (Blackburn and Epel 2017; Hattie 2008; Goleman 1995; Medina 2008). This is a critically important area of study with implications for completely reimagining the nature of modern schooling. However, there also seems to be a great deal of equivocation on what exactly mindfulness is. Does mindfulness work like a binary switch that is either "On" or "Off," or are there more nuanced degrees to mindfulness?

A MINDFULNESS TAXONOMY

In the spirit of contributing to this important dialogue, I would like to share a taxonomy to better define mindfulness. First, here is a working explanation of mindfulness: mindfulness is the discipline of generating meta-feedback to raise awareness of one's feelings and thoughts in the moment and choosing the best action to take in light of both. The explanation I am suggesting contains a nuanced way to enact mindfulness practices at five levels of attainment. Understanding and progressing through each level of this mindfulness taxonomy develops our meta-awareness system, bringing us greater and more sustainable presence in our optimal learning zone.

MINDFULNESS TAXONOMY

5. Meta-Awareness System

4. Metacognition

3. Comprehension

2. Knowledge Acquisition

1. Emotional Regulation

1. *Emotional Regulation*

The first level of mindfulness involves becoming more aware of our emotional state in the moment and then regulating our emotions through the diaphragmatic breath control process. The breathing sequence will help you slow down and reduce the emotional anxiety associated with challenging situations—like deeper learning.

This is so important that it should become part of our daily well-being routines. Think about easing into the consciousness of daily life by taking a few diaphragmatic breaths as soon as you wake up then doing so again before you go to bed at night. You'll find that your emotional state will become more controllable, leading to a greater sense of contentment. As you continue your journey of emotional regulation, you'll begin to experience the serenity that comes with stillness.

2. Knowledge Acquisition

The next level is the knowledge-acquisition phase. This is the level at which we enter new learning mazes when acquiring surface-level information—the new content-specific vocabulary terms, the basic facts, and the larger ideas that are synthesized from those facts. Reflecting in action during the knowledge-acquisition phase allows us to more effectively and efficiently move new superficial content information from working memory to our more permanent memory systems. While this level is important, it is even more important to move from quickly acquired superficial facts toward a deeper understanding and meaning making, which takes us to the next level in this taxonomy.

3. Comprehension

The third level in this meta-system is our comprehension level. At this level we go into the center of the learning maze by more closely examining those surface learning details. We now reflect in action on the similarities and differences of our newly acquired terms, facts, and ideas and then organize them into subordinate categories and superordinate clusters. To do this, we have to enact our default (memory) and inferential (logical) thinking systems to figuratively slay the metaphorical Minotaur of misapprehension. In the process, we are transformed.

We undergo a metamorphosis and exit each learning maze with higher levels of cognizance and consciousness than we had previously. Only then can we proceed to the next level.

4. Metacognition

The fourth level is the metacognition system. This is the level at which we think deeply about our thinking and reflect upon our learning. As discussed in the previous chapter, this is illustrative of reflection *on* action, as it occurs after the learning phase has ended. This approach gives us a retrospective view of our thinking and the learning strategies that we used to bring about our learning. Thinking about both our thinking and learning serves to consolidate the surface- and deeper-level knowledge we have acquired.

5. Meta-Awareness System

The fifth and final level in this taxonomy is the meta-awareness system. This is the level at which we gain a sense of where we are by standing outside ourselves and our circumstances. Engaging in meta-feedback activates our meta-awareness system, allowing us to gain greater perspective on mastering challenging learning tasks while simultaneously being aware of the larger context—the bigger picture of how those tasks relate to our goals and aspirations. We become more fully present in the moment by deeply reflecting on the action as it is happening. This is when we put the final piece of the optimal-performance puzzle together and we enter the zone of optimal learning and performance.

FINDING FLOW

Harnessing the meta-awareness system allows us to be deeply reflective in our actions at the precise moment they are occurring. The meta-awareness system is always available to us. While at first it may seem difficult to attain or activate, the process for enacting the meta-awareness system is really quite simple. All we have to do is engage it. Anyone can do it. It just takes practice. This may seem awkward the first time you try it, but with practice, this ability will be accessible whenever you need it.

Understanding this mindfulness taxonomy will help learners implement meta-feedback strategies to find their optimal learning zones. In his seminal book *Flow: The Psychology of Optimal Experience*, professor Mihaly Csikszentmihalyi (1990) synthesized decades of research on positive psychology to describe a "flow state," in which subjects experienced a type of transcendence-in-action by pursuing optimization in athletics, art, dance, and music. Building upon the ancient Taoist philosophical pillar of "finding flow," Csikszentmihalyi's description of flow complements the concept of an optimal learning zone, where we experience supreme joy in the act of mastering learning something that is just slightly beyond our ability. When we experience such moments, we feel ecstatic; time seems to stand still; and rather than feeling drained, we are energized by the experience (Csikszentmihalyi 1990). Our flow is where we will find our optimal learning zone.

I'd like you to do a visualization exercise to see how easy it is to engage your meta-awareness system. First, you need to get really comfortable doing diaphragmatic breathing exercises, so that you are fully relaxed, alert, and present in the here and now. (Remember: close your eyes and inhale from your diaphragm for the beat of four, hold your breath for four beats, exhale for six beats, pause for two beats, and repeat.) Once you are fully relaxed and alert, keep your eyes closed and visualize physically rising above yourself to gain a larger sense of context. Imagine that you are looking down at yourself in your current location. Visualize your larger environment at this precise moment. If you're outside, what do your surroundings look like from above? If you're inside, how does the room look from a higher vantage point? In essence, what is the bigger picture in which you find yourself?

Once you have the bigger picture captured in your mind's eye, take a few moments and make a sketch of what you have just visualized. The quality of your sketch doesn't matter; just try to capture the essence of this heightened perspective. That's it. That's how you can build the practice of standing outside yourself to ascertain and more fully appreciate the subtle qualities of a unique moment in space and time.

Consider guiding your students to engage in this practice and encourage them to practice at home, before sports events, or ahead of musical performances to get themselves centered in a state of relaxed alertness. Doing so will help them refine this powerful ability to rise above the moment by attaining a more holistic perspective of their experience in time and space: the part and the whole. Your students will find that switching back and forth between these two points of view becomes something that they can do with relative ease.

Now comes the knowledge-transfer piece of the puzzle. Give yourself time to practice transferring this strategy to gain perspective on any learning challenge or performance task you hope to improve. For example, I was most fortunate to earn a doctorate in education leadership from Seattle University. Before every cohort meeting, I would take five minutes to gain perspective on this arduous journey. I would arrive for class early, find an empty room on campus, and then sit there in the dark, practicing my breathing and visualization. I would begin with a gratitude reflection, then I would affirm my capacity to learn and connect this moment to my larger mission of making the world a better place by improving teaching and learning practices. That grounding experience energized me every time. After only five minutes, I would cast aside any doubts I had and get fired up and ready to learn and contribute. Anyone can do this.

Give yourself permission to visualize what you're doing in the moment and how that relates to the bigger picture of your experience and your larger aspirations. Stick with building this capacity, and you'll find that you can gain valuable perspective during the most challenging moments by transcending the moment, rising above the fray, and realizing the awesomeness of the here and now. That is where you'll find your optimal learning zone.

Measuring Your Zone-ness

THE ZONE-NESS SCALE

MASTERY SCORE	INDICATOR
3	Mastering: I am agilely and mindfully implementing this strategy to develop my "zone-ness."
2	Developing: I am close to agilely and mindfully implementing this strategy to develop my "zone-ness."
1	Beginning: I am committed to implementing this strategy to develop my "zone-ness."

Guiding Questions
Meta-Habit #7: Using Meta-Feedback

Regarding the habit of using meta-feedback:

1. Where do you currently fall on the zone-ness scale?
2. Where do you want to be on the zone-ness scale?
3. What will you do to get there?
4. How will you know when you get there?
5. How will you express and represent this to others?

CONCLUSION

The strategy of generating our own meta-feedback builds our innate capacity to learn without limits by allowing us to recognize and engage our meta-awareness system, the overarching executive function of our entire being. Enacting your meta-awareness is a powerful practice that will help you rise above the moment, engage in transcendent pursuits, and get closer and closer to realizing your limitless potential. Learning in the zone is really a function of developing meta-learning habits that help us to move from the superficial and temporary memorization of knowledge toward deeper conceptual understanding, meaning making, and meta-learning.

In the final chapter, we'll bring closure by framing all of the meta-learning habits with a simple but effective mastery scale to help you become more mindful at becoming a meta-learner.

9
ALL TOGETHER NOW

The whole is something else than the sum of its parts, because summing up is a meaningless procedure, whereas the whole–part relationship is meaningful.

—Kurt Koffka

THE BIG PICTURE

Knowing what the seven meta-learning habits are is important, but it's even more important to put the whole of these habits into action and evaluate their impact on your well-being and sense of mastery. When learners put all of these habits into intentional practice, they do in fact create something else: a higher-order interdependent self, if you will. If you and your students have been consistently completing the exercises at the end of each chapter, then you are well on your way (you can go back to any of the chapters and renew your process any time you'd like). Moving from meta-learning theory to action is the most reliable way to realize our optimum learning zone—and our potential for contributive learning without limits.

I'd like to offer a useful meta-learning action plan to help reliably engage your students' meta-learning system. This meta-learning action plan is informed by the final level in Abraham Maslow's hierarchy of needs—physiological needs, safety needs, love and belonging needs, esteem needs, and self-actualization needs (Maslow 1943).

The meta-learning action plan has four stages that have been synthesized from empirical research and practical experience:

1. Self-reflection leads to greater self-regulation.
2. Self-regulation leads to greater self-awareness.
3. Self-awareness leads to greater self-determinism.
4. Self-determinism leads to greater self-actualization.

MAGANA'S META-LEARNING ACTION PLAN

4. Self-determinism leads to greater self-actualization.

3. Self-awareness leads to greater self-determinism.

2. Self-regulation leads to greater self-awareness.

1. Self-reflection leads to greater self-regulation.

1. Self-Reflection Leads to Greater Self-Regulation

A thousand-mile journey begins with the first step. The first step toward self-actualization is self-reflection. Self-reflection is the process of mindfully tending to our emotions and our cognitive thoughts precisely in the moment that we are experiencing those feelings and thoughts. We become far more in tune with ourselves when we take a time-out from our everyday rock and roll to stop, take a breath break, and consider our emotions and thoughts. The dialogue might be something like, "This is me, here and now, feeling great about my progress," or, "Here I am, deciding which option I am going to take to solve this problem." The dialogue itself matters less than stopping, *listening* to our internal voices, and doing the diaphragmatic breathing practice. The simple act of pausing and regulating your breath will give you far greater leverage for strategically regulating your emotional state and your effort—two "currencies" of optimal learning over which we can exert control. With time and consistent practice, you'll find that your highs won't be too high and your lows won't be too low because of *your* actions, not the actions of others.

2. Self-Regulation Leads to Greater Self-Awareness

The awareness of ourselves and our identity as unique human beings is something that we need to own and celebrate. Otherwise, we risk handing the possession of our identities over to others, which in turn puts us in positions of profound inefficacy. On the other hand, greater regulation of our emotional state and thoughts leads to greater self-awareness. This is a process that can include struggle, even hardship. Like a lotus flower rising from the mud to blossom in all its fullness, it is through perseverance that we will deeply know ourselves. The process of consistently regulating our emotions and thoughts by regulating and controlling our breathing has a compounding and positive effect on our sense of self, our well-being, and our capacity for limitless learning.

3. Self-Awareness Leads to Greater Self-Determinism

Gaining greater self-awareness opens the door to self-determinism, or self-efficacy. Self-determinism is the profoundly empowering state in which we fully expect to achieve the goals we have established for ourselves. It is the deeply held belief that we can achieve anything at all. The greater our sense of self-determinism, the more challenging goals and objectives we are able to commit to attaining for ourselves. It all starts with conceiving the end in mind: What is it that you want to achieve next? This is followed by *believing*: you have to deeply believe in your ability to realize whatever you wish to attain. This process ends with *achieving*: whatever you wish to achieve can be realized if you are committed to investing whatever effort is necessary.

4. Self-Determinism Leads to Greater Self-Actualization

With greater self-determinism comes greater levels of self-actualization and the realization of our limitless potential. The funny thing about self-actualization is that it's not a destination. The vision of the proverbial mountaintop on which we can sit in repose, contemplating the fullness of a lifetime of accomplishments, is a myth. The reality is that self-actualization is a journey. It is a process, not a location. The process of continuously pushing past the boundaries of what we know and what we believe we can do is a discipline that moves us closer to fully realizing our limitless potential. It is the transcendent pursuit of chasing the ineffable and discovering ourselves.

PLAYING IN THE BAND

So, what does rock and roll music and limitless learning have in common? As it turns out, quite a bit. Learning how to play rock and roll music helped me learn to identify and develop the seven meta-learning habits. Putting all the seven habits together made a whole that was far greater than each part alone. The sequence of these habits became a blueprint for a lifelong series of fascinating learning journeys. The accumulation of those journeys has brought me to this wonderful moment in my learning life.

I have been implementing these seven learning habits for most of my life now. These habits helped me develop from a shy kid to a contributive learner who is committed to leveraging my learning, knowledge, and skills to make the world a better place by improving the lives of students, teachers, and education leaders. I have dedicated my life to inspiring students to find their own learning zone, and to light the way forward for others who follow them. In 1995, I created and served as principal of Washington State's first CyberSchool—a distributed-learning program that served the needs of students at risk of not completing their high school diploma. The CyberSchool was founded on developing students' meta-learning habits in order for them to find their pathway to optimal learning and self-actualization. By the numbers, CyberSchool was highly successful, achieving graduation rates that far exceeded local and state graduation rates and earning distinction as the first alternative learning program to receive a Washington State Blue Ribbon commendation for academic growth (Javid 2000).

But it's the individual stories of my students—too many to share—that paint a much richer picture of the impact this model has had on my students. A few years ago, I received an email from a former student who attended my CyberSchool. Although I am, like all of us, a work in progress, my student's powerful message eloquently illuminates who I am striving to become as a learner, a teacher, and a contributive member of society:

> Hello Sonny,
>
> I am a former student of yours from CyberSchool in 1998 and 1999. I just wanted to thank you for all that you did. I was quite a mess at the time, and although I fell down several times throughout the years, my getting back up—and more importantly my willingness to learn from my mistakes—is a direct result of what you told/showed/taught me. At the time, you were really the only person I had to go to, or who really cared what I was doing. Even without hindsight or retrospect, I could sense a genuine interest and care for my well-being at that time, which was then, for the most part, nonexistent in my life.

Now with benefit of hindsight, it is more apparent than ever to me that who I am as a person and how I view, analyze, and digest things is a direct result of your persistence and willingness to persevere despite the many (many being a big understatement!) walls and obstacles I placed before you and myself. The tools you gave to me (which even if I didn't utilize at the time, I respected you enough to know their value and hold on to them) have proved invaluable over and over again throughout my life thus far. High school was a rough time for me, both in and out of school, and I feel that my home life and the personal choices I made dictated who I was and, ultimately what I became while at school. Which is what landed me in your CyberSchool, eventually.

I came into your room full of spite and desperation, which was masked by a cocky attitude and absolutely no respect whatsoever. In the time that I was at CyberSchool I feel that I learned more from you than I ever did anywhere else. Ever. I believe it stuck with me and ultimately changed my entire outlook because the things I took from you weren't from a book or lesson plan. I learned about life, about kindness, about respecting others, and why I should be doing so. I learned about owning up to my mistakes (I will never forget you catching me plagiarizing the subway essay!) and taking responsibility for them, without having to know the outcome and in trusting that doing the right thing will ultimately get me so much further. I learned to not blame everyone else for my mistakes. I learned to realize my potential and believe in my potential with reckless abandon. I learned that it's okay to be upset and to hurt and to properly analyze and digest those feelings instead of acting on them. I really could go on forever.

What was most important to me is that I learned how to be a man. At the time when I met you, my father had placed a restraining order on me. I was doing drugs. Yet I managed to go to your class every single day, and I firmly believe it was because of that. I had nothing positive in my life, no family at the time, no role model. And here you came out of nowhere and filled that role in my life, with no benefit to yourself. I am so happy that I was able to see that back then and carry it with me all this time. It is truly the foundation for who I've become today. It is the reason I see all this beauty around me, have faith in people, and am able to appreciate the smallest of things, even when things are at their worst and despair should be immense.

I absolutely love who I am as a person, I love what my values are, and I absolutely believe in myself without question. Who I became has changed everything in my life. I have real friends, genuine relationships, and my father and I are tighter than ever. So many negative things have happened throughout the years that I feel normally would break a person, however I now see that every situation just makes me stronger. I feel, with unwavering certainty, that you are directly responsible for this, and so I just wanted to thank you, from the bottom of my heart, for all that you did and continue to do to this day.

You believed in me and stuck with me when everyone else gave up, including myself. So again, thank you. Even if you don't remember me, you should feel extremely good because you affected at least one person's life. What I've learned over the years because of you is that each and every life is as beautiful as the next and as beautiful as them all as a whole. So, to be responsible for making that happen... it's quite an incredible feat, my friend. Thank you, again, for everything. Your advice and caring dedication will continue to shape my future and allow me to see the beauty in everything and everyone, and more importantly to teach them how to see the same.

With the highest regard and admiration,
Chris Siegel
CyberSchool Class of 1999

This email was totally unexpected and still touches my heart in ways that I simply can't describe. My vision for CyberSchool was to create and sustain an experiential learning environment conducive to helping at-risk students realize that meta-learning doesn't just happen in classrooms, but can—and should—take place anywhere, anytime, and for the entirety of one's life. Lifelong love of limitless learning is our birthright.

THE ROAD AHEAD

It's important to consider that meta-learning is not a destination, but a never-ending journey, one filled with wondrous discoveries about ourselves and the infinitely connected world of which we are an inextricable part. This may seem intimidating, but upon deeper reflection, one realizes that this perspective gives one the freedom to take risks, to fail, to learn from those failures, and to try again. In that time-honored tradition, we develop the habit of learning how we learn best.

We are now living in a world where volatility, uncertainty, chaos, and ambiguity are the new normal. If Alvin Toffler was right, and I think he was, then meta-learning—learning how to optimize how we learn, unlearn, and relearn—is *the* essential literacy for the twenty-first century and beyond. At this moment in history, humans have access to information twenty-four hours a day, three hundred and sixty-five days a year. However, we are also far more susceptible to misinformation, manipulation, propaganda, and harmful conspiracy theories than at any other time in human history. This only underscores the importance of developing students' capacity to learn what is useful, unlearn what isn't, and relearn with confidence, optimism, and hope for building a better future for all.

The most important technologies we have at our immediate disposal are our human hearts and minds. That's where we find our optimal learning zones; it's the place where we find what a true love of learning feels like. If we're lucky, we'll do it for the rest of our lives. If we're really lucky, we get to invite as many other people as possible to fall in love with learning. That's where the zone is—finding your optimal learning zone, and then helping others find theirs. The road ahead beckons. Enjoy every step…and keep practicing!

REFERENCES

Benson, H. 1975. *The Relaxation Response*. New York: HarperCollins.

Benson, H., and W. Proctor. 1987. *Your Maximum Mind*. New York: Crown Publishing.

Benson, H., and W. Proctor. 2010. *Relaxation Revolution: The Science and Genetics of Mind Body Healing*. New York: Simon & Schuster.

Blackburn, E., and E. Epel. 2017. *The Telomere Effect: A Revolutionary Approach to Living Younger, Healthier, Longer*. New York: Grand Central Publishing.

Bransford, J., A. L. Brown, and R. R. Cocking. 2000. *How People Learn: Brain, Mind, Experience and School*. Washington, DC: National Academy Press.

Breuning, L. 2018. "Stimulating Dopamine, Serotonin, Oxytocin and Endorphin by Learning How They're Stimulated in Animals." *Journal of Medical-Clinical Research & Reviews* 2, no. 4. www.researchgate.net/publication/330782045_Stimulating_Dopamine_Serotonin_Oxytocin_and_Endorphin_by_Learning_How_They%27re_Stimulated_in_Animals.

Bruner, J. S. 1968. *Toward a Theory of Instruction*. Cambridge, MA: Harvard University Press.

Csikszentmihalyi, M. 1990. *Flow: The Psychology of Optimal Experience*. New York: Harper & Row.

Dewey, J. 1938. *Experience and Education.* New York: Kappa Delta Pi.

Goleman, D. 1995. *Emotional Intelligence.* New York: Bantam Books.

Harari, Y. N. 2015. *Sapiens: A Brief History of Humankind.* New York: Harper Perennial.

Haystead, M., and S. Magana. 2013. "Using Technology to Enhance the Art and Science of Teaching Framework: A Descriptive Case Study." Denver, CO: Marzano Research.

Hattie, J. 2008. *Visible Learning: A Synthesis of over 800 Meta-Analyses Relating to Achievement.* New York: Routledge.

Hattie, J. 2012. *Visible Learning for Teachers: Maximizing Impact on Learning.* New York: Routledge.

Javid, M. 2000. "Portrait of a Symbiotic Model for a Working Cyberschool: A Two-Year Case Study of a Technology Driven Public High School." Unpublished doctoral dissertation, Seattle University.

Laozi and Chan, W. (1963). *The Way of Lao Tzu (Tao-te ching).* Upper Saddle River, NJ: Prentice-Hall.

Magana, S. 2016. "Enhancing the Art and Science of Teaching with Technology: A Model for Improving Learning for All Students." Unpublished doctoral dissertation, Seattle University.

Magana, S. 2017. *Disruptive Classroom Technologies: A Framework for Innovation in Education.* Thousand Oaks, CA: Corwin Press.

Magana, S. 2019. "Disruptive Classroom Technologies Research Review." In *Oxford Research Encyclopedia of Education.* doi.org/10.1093/acrefore/9780190264093.013.423.

Magana, S., and R. J. Marzano. 2014. *Enhancing the Art and Science of Teaching with Technology.* Bloomington, IN: Solution Tree Press.

Marzano, R. J. 2007. *The Art and Science of Teaching: A Comprehensive Framework for Effective Instruction.* Alexandria, VA: Association for Supervision and Curriculum Development.

Marzano, R. J., D. J. Pickering, and J. E. Pollock. 2001. *Classroom Instruction That Works: Research-Based Strategies for Increasing Student Achievement.* Alexandria, VA: Association for Supervision and Curriculum Development.

Maslow, A. H. 1943. "A Theory of Human Motivation." *Psychological Review* 50, no. 4: 430–437.

Medina, J. 2008. *Brain Rules: 12 Principles for Surviving and Thriving at Work, Home and School.* Seattle, WA: Pear Press.

Murray, W. H. 1951. *The Scottish Himalayan Expedition.* London: Dent.

Vygotsky, L. 1978. *Mind in Society.* Cambridge, MA: Harvard University Press.

ACKNOWLEDGMENTS

Finding and maintaining one's optimal learning zone is a team sport, and so is writing a book. I wish to express my gratitude to all of my former students at ACES Alternative High School and ACES CyberSchool—in particular Wendy Smith and Chris Siegel for their gracious contribution to this work. I am deeply grateful to Dr. Robert J. Marzano and Professor John Hattie for their gracious guidance and support. I would also like to thank Dr. Mike Chaix, Dr. Robert McCollum, Dr. Cathy Reznicek, Dr. Julie Judd, Dr. Carla Taughler-Aranda, Dr. Mike McCormick, Rick Oser, Dana Thompson, Faysel Bell, Aaron Jones, Christie Cuevas, Jennifer Goodman, Heather Esposito, Allison Staffin, Jay Sorensen, Alice Keeler, my esteemed colleagues Marlena Hebern and Jon Corippo, Shelley and Dave Burgess, and the entire team at DBCI for believing in my vision for this "In the Zone" series. Next up: *Teaching in the Zone*!

ABOUT DR. SONNY MAGANA

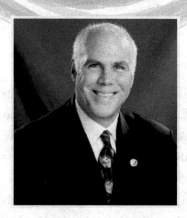

DR. ANTHONY J. "SONNY" MAGANA is a digital-age learning pioneer. In 1995, Sonny created and served as principal of Washington State's first CyberSchool—which is still serving the needs of at-risk students. An award-winning teacher and researcher, Sonny authored the best-selling book *Disruptive Classroom Technologies*, which introduced the T3 Framework as a next-generation pedagogy for the modern era. The T3 Framework was shown to reliably accelerate student learning and was inducted into the *Oxford Research Encyclopedia of Education*. His work has been called "visionary and inspirational" by Dr. Robert Marzano, "a brilliant breakthrough in our understanding and use of technology for learning" by Professor Michael Fullan, and "a major step forward in our understanding of the Visible Learning model" by Professor John Hattie.

An avid yoga practitioner, musician, and mountaineer, Sonny was awarded the Milken Family Foundation Educator Award, the inaugural Washington Governor's Commendation for Educational Excellence, and the Global Education Leadership Award from EdTech Digest, which named him one of the top influencers in education. He holds a bachelor of science degree from Stockton University, a master of education degree from City University, and an administrative credential and doctorate in educational leadership from Seattle University. He has summited the highest peaks in his home state of Washington, where he continues to pursue his passion, the outdoors.

MORE FROM

Since 2012, DBCI has published books that inspire and equip educators to be their best. For more information on our titles or to purchase bulk orders for your school, district, or book study, visit DaveBurgessConsulting.com/DBCIbooks.

THE *LIKE A PIRATE*™ SERIES

Teach Like a PIRATE by Dave Burgess
eXPlore Like a PIRATE by Michael Matera
Learn Like a PIRATE by Paul Solarz
Plan Like a PIRATE by Dawn M. Harris
Play Like a PIRATE by Quinn Rollins
Run Like a PIRATE by Adam Welcome
Tech Like a PIRATE by Matt Miller

LEAD *LIKE A PIRATE*™ SERIES

Lead Like a PIRATE by Shelley Burgess and Beth Houf
Balance Like a PIRATE by Jessica Cabeen, Jessica Johnson, and Sarah Johnson
Lead beyond Your Title by Nili Bartley
Lead with Appreciation by Amber Teamann and Melinda Miller
Lead with Culture by Jay Billy
Lead with Instructional Rounds by Vicki Wilson
Lead with Literacy by Mandy Ellis
She Leads by Dr. Rachael George and Majalise W. Tolan

LEADERSHIP & SCHOOL CULTURE

Beyond the Surface of Restorative Practices by Marisol Rerucha
Change the Narrative by Henry J. Turner and Kathy Lopes
Choosing to See by Pamela Seda and Kyndall Brown
Culturize by Jimmy Casas
Discipline Win by Andy Jacks
Escaping the School Leader's Dunk Tank by Rebecca Coda and Rick Jetter
Fight Song by Kim Bearden
From Teacher to Leader by Starr Sackstein
If the Dance Floor Is Empty, Change the Song by Joe Clark
The Innovator's Mindset by George Couros
It's OK to Say "They" by Christy Whittlesey
Kids Deserve It! by Todd Nesloney and Adam Welcome
Let Them Speak by Rebecca Coda and Rick Jetter
The Limitless School by Abe Hege and Adam Dovico
Live Your Excellence by Jimmy Casas
Next-Level Teaching by Jonathan Alsheimer
The Pepper Effect by Sean Gaillard
Principaled by Kate Barker, Kourtney Ferrua, and Rachael George
The Principled Principal by Jeffrey Zoul and Anthony McConnell
Relentless by Hamish Brewer
The Secret Solution by Todd Whitaker, Sam Miller, and Ryan Donlan
Start. Right. Now. by Todd Whitaker, Jeffrey Zoul, and Jimmy Casas
Stop. Right. Now. by Jimmy Casas and Jeffrey Zoul
Teachers Deserve It by Rae Hughart and Adam Welcome
Teach Your Class Off by CJ Reynolds
They Call Me "Mr. De" by Frank DeAngelis
Thrive through the Five by Jill M. Siler
Unmapped Potential by Julie Hasson and Missy Lennard
When Kids Lead by Todd Nesloney and Adam Dovico
Word Shift by Joy Kirr
Your School Rocks by Ryan McLane and Eric Lowe

TECHNOLOGY & TOOLS

50 Things to Go Further with Google Classroom by Alice Keeler and Libbi Miller
50 Things You Can Do with Google Classroom by Alice Keeler and Libbi Miller
140 Twitter Tips for Educators by Brad Currie, Billy Krakower, and Scott Rocco
Block Breaker by Brian Aspinall
Building Blocks for Tiny Techies by Jamila "Mia" Leonard
Code Breaker by Brian Aspinall
The Complete EdTech Coach by Katherine Goyette and Adam Juarez
Control Alt Achieve by Eric Curts
The Esports Education Playbook by Chris Aviles, Steve Isaacs, Christine Lion-Bailey, and Jesse Lubinsky
Google Apps for Littles by Christine Pinto and Alice Keeler
Master the Media by Julie Smith
Raising Digital Leaders by Jennifer Casa-Todd
Reality Bytes by Christine Lion-Bailey, Jesse Lubinsky, and Micah Shippee, PhD
Sail the 7 Cs with Microsoft Education by Becky Keene and Kathi Kersznowski
Shake Up Learning by Kasey Bell
Social LEADia by Jennifer Casa-Todd
Stepping Up to Google Classroom by Alice Keeler and Kimberly Mattina
Teaching Math with Google Apps by Alice Keeler and Diana Herrington
Teachingland by Amanda Fox and Mary Ellen Weeks
Teaching with Google Jamboard by Alice Keeler and Kimberly Mattina

TEACHING METHODS & MATERIALS

All 4s and 5s by Andrew Sharos
Boredom Busters by Katie Powell
The Classroom Chef by John Stevens and Matt Vaudrey
The Collaborative Classroom by Trevor Muir
Copyrighteous by Diana Gill
CREATE by Bethany J. Petty

Deploying EduProtocols by Kim Voge, with Jon Corippo and Marlena Hebern
Ditch That Homework by Matt Miller and Alice Keeler
Ditch That Textbook by Matt Miller
Don't Ditch That Tech by Matt Miller, Nate Ridgway, and Angelia Ridgway
EDrenaline Rush by John Meehan
Educated by Design by Michael Cohen, The Tech Rabbi
The EduProtocol Field Guide by Marlena Hebern and Jon Corippo
The EduProtocol Field Guide: Book 2 by Marlena Hebern and Jon Corippo
The EduProtocol Field Guide: Math Edition by Lisa Nowakowski and Jeremiah Ruesch
Expedition Science by Becky Schnekser
Frustration Busters by Katie Powell
Fully Engaged by Michael Matera and John Meehan
Game On? Brain On! by Lindsay Portnoy, PhD
Guided Math AMPED by Reagan Tunstall
Innovating Play by Jessica LaBar-Twomy and Christine Pinto
Instructional Coaching Connection by Nathan Lang-Raad
Instant Relevance by Denis Sheeran
Keeping the Wonder by Jenna Copper, Ashley Bible, Abby Gross, and Staci Lamb
LAUNCH by John Spencer and A.J. Juliani
Make Learning MAGICAL by Tisha Richmond
Pass the Baton by Kathryn Finch and Theresa Hoover
Project-Based Learning Anywhere by Lori Elliott
Pure Genius by Don Wettrick
The Revolution by Darren Ellwein and Derek McCoy
Shift This! by Joy Kirr
Skyrocket Your Teacher Coaching by Michael Cary Sonbert
Spark Learning by Ramsey Musallam
Sparks in the Dark by Travis Crowder and Todd Nesloney
Table Talk Math by John Stevens
Unpack Your Impact by Naomi O'Brien and LaNesha Tabb

The Wild Card by Hope and Wade King
Writefully Empowered by Jacob Chastain
The Writing on the Classroom Wall by Steve Wyborney
You Are Poetry by Mike Johnston

INSPIRATION, PROFESSIONAL GROWTH & PERSONAL DEVELOPMENT

Be REAL by Tara Martin
Be the One for Kids by Ryan Sheehy
The Coach ADVenture by Amy Illingworth
Creatively Productive by Lisa Johnson
Educational Eye Exam by Alicia Ray
The EduNinja Mindset by Jennifer Burdis
Empower Our Girls by Lynmara Colón and Adam Welcome
Finding Lifelines by Andrew Grieve and Andrew Sharos
The Four O'Clock Faculty by Rich Czyz
How Much Water Do We Have? by Pete and Kris Nunweiler
P Is for Pirate by Dave and Shelley Burgess
A Passion for Kindness by Tamara Letter
The Path to Serendipity by Allyson Apsey
Rogue Leader by Rich Czyz
Sanctuaries by Dan Tricarico
Saving Sycamore by Molly B. Hudgens
The SECRET SAUCE by Rich Czyz
Shattering the Perfect Teacher Myth by Aaron Hogan
Stories from Webb by Todd Nesloney
Talk to Me by Kim Bearden
Teach Better by Chad Ostrowski, Tiffany Ott, Rae Hughart, and Jeff Gargas
Teach Me, Teacher by Jacob Chastain
Teach, Play, Learn! by Adam Peterson
The Teachers of Oz by Herbie Raad and Nathan Lang-Raad
TeamMakers by Laura Robb and Evan Robb
Through the Lens of Serendipity by Allyson Apsey
The Zen Teacher by Dan Tricarico

CHILDREN'S BOOKS

Beyond Us by Aaron Polansky
Cannonball In by Tara Martin
Dolphins in Trees by Aaron Polansky
I Can Achieve Anything by MoNique Waters
I Want to Be a Lot by Ashley Savage
Micah's Big Question by Naomi O'Brien
The Princes of Serendip by Allyson Apsey
Ride with Emilio by Richard Nares
The Wild Card Kids by Hope and Wade King
Zom-Be a Design Thinker by Amanda Fox

CPSIA information can be obtained
at www.ICGtesting.com
Printed in the USA
BVHW030356150722
642102BV00008B/17